# DR. HERBERT BENSON, WHO TAUGHT US *THE RELAXATION RESPONSE,* NOW HELPS YOU DEVELOP *YOUR MAXIMUM MIND*

"Dr. Benson continues to enrich our lives
with his valid and valuable insights."
Rabbi Harold Kushner,
author of *When Bad Things Happen To Good People*

"The author who taught us how to relax
now guides us to reshaping our minds
and letting them be open to change…
A master key to improving human performance
and enhancing spiritual development."
Rev. Robert H. Schuller, author of
*Tough Times Never Last But Tough People Do!*

"Herbert Benson describes
the nature and range of the inner resources
of human beings
and shows how they can be put to work.
The result is a valuable and practical guidebook
in the uses of human powers."
Norman Cousins,
author of *The Healing Heart*

*Other Avon Books by*
**Herbert Benson, M.D.**

THE RELAXATION RESPONSE
*with Miriam Z. Klipper*

# Your Maximum Mind

HERBERT BENSON, M.D.

with William Proctor

Because this page cannot legibly accommodate the permissions acknowledgments, these appear on the page opposite.



AVON BOOKS
A division of
The Hearst Corporation
1350 Avenue of the Americas
New York, New York 10019


Published by arrangement with Random House, Inc.
Library of Congress Catalog Card Number: 87-9969
ISBN: 0-380-70664-4



First Avon Books Printing: February 1989



Printed in Canada

UNV 10 9 8 7 6 5

*Grateful acknowledgment is made to the following for permission to reprint previously published material:*

Bantam Books, Inc.: Excerpts from *The Aerobics Program for Total Well-Being* by Kenneth H. Cooper, M.D., M.P.H. Copyright © 1982 by Kenneth H. Cooper. Reprinted by permission of Bantam Books, Inc. All Rights Reserved.

Dodd, Mead & Company, Inc.: Excerpt from "The Law of the Yukon" from *The Collected Poems of Robert Service.* Copyright 1909 by Dodd, Mead & Company, Inc. Reprinted by permission of Dodd, Mead & Company, Inc., and Feinman & Krasilovsky as agent for the Estate of Robert William Service.

Harcourt Brace Jovanovich, Inc. and Faber and Faber Limited Publishers: Excerpt from "Burnt Norton" in *Four Quartets* by T.S. Eliot, copyright 1943 by T.S. Eliot; renewed 1971 by Esme Valerie Eliot. Reprinted by permission of the publishers.

Prentice Hall, Inc.: Excerpt from *The Power of Positive Thinking* by Norman Vincent Peale. Copyright 1952 © 1956, 1986. Used by permission of the publisher, Prentice-Hall, Inc. Englewood Cliffs, NJ.

United Feature Syndicate, Inc.: Excerpts from *It's Possible* by Robert H. Schuller. Reprinted by permission.

Warner Bros. Music: Excerpt from the lyrics to "Pack Up Your Troubles in Your Old Kit Bag" by Felix Powell and George Asaf. Copyright 1915 Warner Bros., Inc. (Renewed). All Rights Reserved. Used by Permission.

TO

**Arman Simone**

AND

**Joseph J. Schildkraut**

*with gratitude and in friendship*

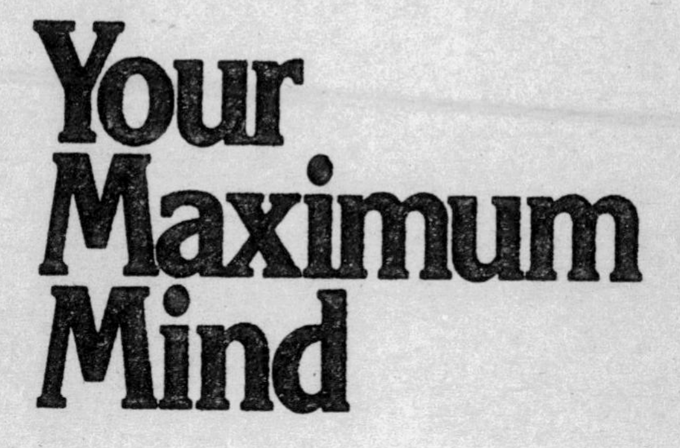
Your
Maximum
Mind

# *Foreword*

This book brings together findings from more than twenty years of my research, teaching and clinical activities at the Harvard Medical School and also at several of its major teaching affiliates. In making my argument, I've relied on evidence from the often disparate fields of clinical medicine, physiology, psychiatry, psychology, religion, philosophy and athletics. Together, this interdisciplinary information helps define a remarkable human capacity, your Maximum Mind. This book also presents practical guidelines to achieve beneficial results.

As research into the widespread manifestations of the Maximum Mind continues, new data may lead to new realizations. But our own compelling results with many patients, coupled with a unifying scientific framework, now justify presenting the Principle of the Maximum Mind for general consideration and use.

The Principle of the Maximum Mind has potentially life-transforming capabilities, and for this reason, it's necessary to take certain precautions. In particular, if any reader decides to make use of the Principle for medical or spiritual matters, he or she should proceed under the direction of what we have called a "maximum mind guide."

This guide should be a health professional if your main interest is in improving your health. For example, if you choose to apply the Principle of the Maximum Mind to the treatment of hypertension or any other medical illness, you should do so only with the approval and subsequent supervision of your physician. Similarly, a minister, rabbi, priest or other trained religious adviser would be an appropriate guide if your goal is a changed spiritual life.

Sometimes a maximum mind guide may be helpful if you want to use the Principle of the Maximum Mind to achieve expertise in some challenging area of knowledge; for example, you may want to find a language expert to monitor your progress with a foreign language. Or you may want to talk to an athletic adviser if enhanced fitness or athletic performance is your objective. For less sensitive or less difficult matters, you may find you can proceed without a guide and simply rely on readings such as those cited in the phase two sections of this book.

All case presentations are based on real individuals. Their names, their sex or nonessential circumstances have been altered to ensure anonymity.

I am very grateful to Nancy E. MacKinnon, Anna

K. Arthur, Irene L. Goodale, Anne Jacobs, Terry A. Bard, Frederick Commoner, Gregory C. Benson and Fafa Demasio for their excellent assistance in the preparation of this book. I am also appreciative of the contributions of Dr. George S. Everly, Jr., Robert L. Allen and Samuel S. Myers, who indirectly aided this work through our discussions and collaborative research projects. For his counsel, I thank Robert E. Cowden, III. The interest and suggestions of my good friend T. George Harris have been most welcome and useful. Once again, I am ever indebted to Marilyn, my wife, for her superb advice, patience and support.

Aspects of this book were made possible by funds given by the John E. Fetzer Foundation, Arman Simone, the Ruth Mott Fund, and William K. Coors. I also gratefully acknowledge the financial support of Laurance S. Rockefeller, George S. Warburg and Francis X. Meaney. The research and development of the book were also funded, in part, by grants from the United States Public Health Service (HL-22727 and HL-07374); from the National Science Foundation (NSF INT 8016982); and from the American Institute of Indian Studies.

**H.B.**
Boston
June 1987

# Contents

# PART I

• • •

# *The Secret to Remolding Your Mind, Your Habits and Your Life*

# 1. Can You Really Change the Way You Think and Act?

The Dalai Lama, a great student of the human mind as well as the spiritual leader of the Tibetan Buddhists, once said, "We human beings have a developed brain and limitless potential. Since even wild animals can gradually be trained with patience, the human mind also can gradually be trained, step by step. With patience, you can come to know this through your own experience."

As the Dalai Lama suggests, the brain is a most wonderful part of the human anatomy. Yet it's also most mysterious. There's so much we don't know, and perhaps may never know, about the way our minds work. But gradually, some of the mysteries are being unveiled—to the great advantage of modern medicine *and* to the benefit of anyone who wants to improve his or her personal potential.

How often have you criticized yourself because you felt you weren't living up to your full potential? How many times have you said, "If I could only

- get rid of this bad habit;
- overcome this health problem;
- become a more productive person;
- be more disciplined;
- develop expertise in this skill or that body of knowledge?"

Most of us want to improve. We want to better ourselves, to move up to another plateau of achievement. But many times, something seems to block our way.

Think back on your own aspirations over the last few years. How many self-help programs have you tried—or wanted to try?

Perhaps you've always wanted to go to night school and work toward a graduate degree. Or maybe your primary goal is to do some studying on your own—say, in a foreign language that you've always wanted to master. On the other hand, you may have thought seriously about embarking on an independent reading and study program in great works of literature which you missed in your younger years.

Then again, your interests, and frustrations, may center more in the health and fitness area. Perhaps you're moving into your thirties, forties or beyond, and you see that the physical profile you were so proud of has disappeared. You know you're ten or twenty pounds overweight, and you've desperately wanted, and occasionally tried, to take off those extra pounds—all to no avail.

Obviously, a reasonable antidote to your poor fitness could be an exercise program—a regular regimen of sit-ups, push-ups, leg stretches or whatever. But so often you've launched such a fitness program, only to fall back into your old, sedentary way of life.

On the other hand, developing more discipline at the office may be your major aspiration. Perhaps you're deeply concerned about whether you're positioning yourself properly to get an attractive promotion. To achieve this goal, you know you'll have to improve in several areas where you're deficient—say in the financial and accounting fields. But try as you may, you can't seem to get started on a program to turn these deficiencies of yours into assets.

Or perhaps your main concern is your spiritual side. In the rush to succeed in the world and keep your personal and social life going at the maximum, you've neglected the deeper levels of human existence. In short, you want to know more about God; about the teachings of your church or synagogue; and about pressing theological and spiritual questions you've never been able to answer adequately. You may also wish to experience other levels of spiritual awareness. But these concerns, which you acknowledge are very important, keep getting put aside because you can't seem to make time for them.

We've all felt these frustrations and pressures as we find ourselves unable to live up to personal expectations. In the last analysis, we feel "stuck in a rut." We can't seem to shake the old, bad habits or health problems that have controlled us in the past and prevented us from moving ahead to acquire new, beneficial forms of self-discipline. Too often, we're tempted to say, "Well, I guess there's nothing I can do to change myself or overcome my limitations. I'm just made this way, and I may as well accept it."

Nonsense. My research has convinced me that there is hope for meaningful change in your life:

- you can break through those old bad habits;
- you can alleviate many illnesses that have been plaguing you;
- you can alter unproductive ways of thinking and develop new disciplines that will help you realize your full potential; and
- you can embark on a truly transformed way of living.

How is this possible?

The principle is something I've come to call maximizing your mind—a process directly related to the Relaxation Response.

The Relaxation Response has been the focal point of my own medical research and clinical practice for the last twenty years. For those of you who are unfamiliar with this work, the Relaxation Response refers to the ability of the body to enter into a scientifically definable state characterized by an overall reduction of the speed of the body's metabolism, lowered blood pressure, decreased rate of breathing, lowered heart rate, and more prominent, slower brain waves.

The Relaxation Response has its most powerful impact when combined with what I've called the Faith Factor. This involves eliciting the Response in the context of a deeply held set of personal, religious or philosophical beliefs.

Until now, I've recommended that the Relaxation Response be used primarily to combat the harmful and uncomfortable effects of stress on the mind and body. Recent observations, however, show there is considerably more to this phenomenon.

In fact, we've found that the Relaxation Response also acts, in a rather extraordinary fashion, as a kind of door to a renewed mind and changed life. It can enable you to change even the most deeply ingrained bad habits. It can enable you to develop new, beneficial disciplines, and enhance your health in ways which you had always felt were beyond your grasp. In short, the Relaxation Response is the first and probably most crucial step in making practically any self-help program work successfully for you.

How, exactly, can the Relaxation Response act as the catalyst to renew your mind? How can it help you change your habits, improve your health and transform your life?

### *Channels of the Mind*

Over the years, you develop "circuits" and "channels" of thought in your brain. These are physical pathways which control the way you think, the way you act, and often, the way you feel. Many times, these pathways or habits become so fixed that they turn into what I call "wiring." In other words, the circuits or channels become so deeply ingrained that it seems almost impossible to transform them. They actually become part of your brain; they are part of *you*.

The functioning of the brain is too complicated and our knowledge is too limited to sum up its workings in simple terms. But researchers have determined that some basic rules of thumb are generally valid. And the practical implications are far-reaching.

Neurophysiologists like Drs. Roger Sperry and Michael S. Gazzaniga have been investigating so-called "split brain" phenomena involving the activities of the left and right hemispheres of the brain. Among other things, they have demonstrated that the left hemisphere of the brain is largely responsible for controlling much of the analytical, inferential and language-related skills and thinking processes. The right hemisphere is the area in which much of the intuitive, artistic and creative thinking resides.*

Consider, for example, the question of how you can change a bad habit or acquire a new skill. By various logical—but often inaccurate—inferences, your left brain may in effect "tell" you that certain beneficial changes in your personality, skills and habits are impossible. And despite the inaccuracies, you'll believe what you're "hearing." Why? Because, more often than not, there will be little internal argument or opposition from your right hemisphere.

In very practical terms, then, it's largely the established circuits of the left side of our brain that are telling us, "You can't change your way of living. . . .Your

* When we talk about left-brain and right-brain functions, I'll always be referring to right-handed people. For a left-handed person, the functions of the two hemispheres of the brain are reversed.

bad habits are forever. . . .You're just made in a certain way, and you have to live with that fact."

That simply is not true.

Significant, even dramatic change *is* possible. How? By eliciting the Relaxation Response through meditation, prayer or other techniques, you can set the stage for important mind- and habit-altering brain change. Furthermore, you'll be able to break free into a new way of life, where you're maximizing many of your inherent capabilities.

In more specific terms, this change can occur as a result of a different type of communication between the left and right sides of your brain. Scientific research has shown that electrical activity between the left and right sides of the brain becomes coordinated during certain kinds of meditation or prayer. My own experience with patients has demonstrated that, through these processes, the mind definitely becomes more capable of being altered and having its capacities maximized.

To the end of producing beneficial change, we'll discuss in the following pages how you can increase your chances to:

- succeed with self-help programs;
- strengthen self-discipline;
- achieve difficult exercise and athletic goals;
- increase your creativity and decision-making skills;
- enhance the effects of psychotherapy;
- decrease medications you may be taking;
- overcome your irrational fears;
- diminish the tyranny of pain in your life;
- break your unhealthy and destructive thought patterns; and
- support and expand your spiritual life.

### *Some Basic Ground Rules for Reading This Book*

Before we go any further, I'd like to lay down some basic ground rules about how to approach the subject of renewing your mind.

First of all, most of the force for change in your life will come as you learn to use portions of your brain in different ways. In particular, you'll have to learn to utilize more fully the activity of the intuitive, creative side of your mind—that is, the *right* hemisphere of your brain.

Some immediate problems arise when anyone attempts to teach you how to expand the possibilities for the use of the right side of your brain. Language—the primary tool of instruction—is itself largely a function of the *left* hemisphere. By definition, then, the workings of the right side of your brain can't be put into words as easily as those of the left side.

In fact, as you know, you can't put some things into words at all. You've encountered many such inexpressible experiences: a stunning, orange-red sunset; the inner thrill which comes with achieving some long-sought goal; a profound positive—or negative—reaction to some person or event; a mental "light bulb" which suddenly illuminates your mind with a creative idea or concept; a life-changing mystical or spiritual insight; an intuition or "sense" that something is right or wrong; an experience of being in love.

Of course, all these things are real. In fact, they're often *more* real than thoughts or encounters you can reduce quite precisely to words. Somehow, these profound events remain ineffable. They defy ordinary logic, analysis or description.

Similarly, much of what we'll be discussing in the following pages will stay, at least in part, beyond the ability of our minds to wrap up into neat verbal analytical packages. In fact, reducing everything to words is impossible because of the way our brains are constructed. Yet even when the words escape us, we must remember the central point: The brain possesses an inherent capacity to change, a capacity which I've called the Principle of Your Maximum Mind. You actually have the power to alter dramatically the way you think and act.

Because many of the concepts in this book can only be *experienced* in a nonverbal way, I want to propose an optional way of reading this book. Certainly, you can read this book as you would any other—and I think you'll be able to get a great deal out of it with this approach. But if one of your main goals is to break away from a purely analytical approach to life, the optional strategy is designed to help you release the Principle of Your Maximum Mind as you read. You may actually find that as you read the book, you're able to use the Principle to understand the Principle!

So here's what I suggest.

First, read through the book much as you would any other book, but with this difference: Try eliciting the Relaxation Response at the beginning of each of your reading sessions. (The technique is reviewed on page 22.) That way you'll open yourself to the possibility for significant change in your life, as the left and right sides of your brain coordinate more readily with each other. This approach, by the way, will be quite appropriate for those who are already familiar with the elicitation of the Relaxation Response. This method will of course take a little more time than just reading the book through from start to finish. But the potential benefits you can experience in transforming your personal habits and the patterns of your mind will more than justify the extra time.

Imagine some of the possibilities: You may actually begin to learn a new language, hone a long-desired athletic skill or eliminate a phobia or other medical problem—as you're reading this book. And the key to these life-changing experiences may simply be your willingness to extend your reading sessions slightly.

If you're *really* ambitious, you might try a somewhat more rigorous technique. When you come to a section of the book which strikes a deeply responsive chord in you, try reading that section several times before you go on. Also, at the beginning of each reading, elicit the Relaxation Response. That will help you start your creative, mind-renewing powers operating at more intensive levels.

I've designed this book to make it easy for you to return to it repeatedly as you continue to try to change or improve various aspects of your life in the future. Right now, you may perhaps be interested primarily in developing a more positive attitude toward life. Later you may wish to develop a regular exercise program. Whatever your objectives, you can return to the particular section of the book most meaningful to you at the time. Over a period of days, weeks or even months, I'd suggest you read over the relevant section of the book regularly, just after you've elicited the Relaxation Response.

As you'll see, the elicitation of the Relaxation Response—and the period which immediately follows—

are very important in your efforts to transform your mind and your life. This is the time when I believe you're most receptive to altering your established mental circuits—and achieving beneficial change. It is a time when your mental "slate" is cleaner and more open. So just after your meditation or prayer, it's important to focus immediately on things which relate to the life-changing goals you've chosen, as we'll discuss in subsequent chapters. Soon you'll find your thought patterns shifting, sometimes quite subtly, into more productive paths: Changed actions and a changed life will follow. The implications are exciting and even staggering when you learn how to incorporate the Principle of Your Maximum Mind fully into your life.

Now, before we get into any more of the practical implications of these concepts, let's examine a little more closely what we know about the scientific basis for the Principle of Your Maximum Mind.

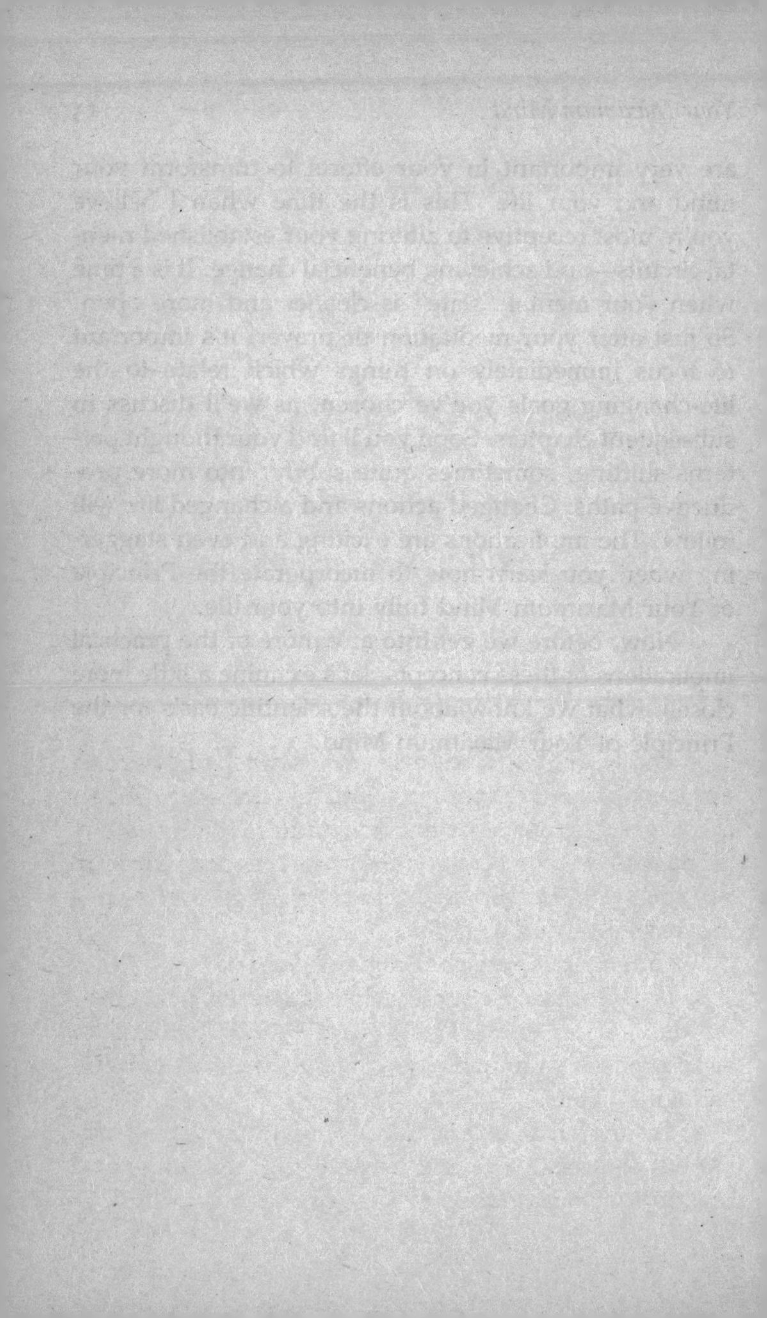

# 2.

## *The Principle of Your Maximum Mind*

The workings of the human brain remain beyond our complete understanding and comprehension. We've made giant strides in comprehending the physiology of the brain and its capacity to control the many intricate workings of our bodies and thought patterns. Yet there's much we still don't know.

For example, we continue to wonder:

- Is the mind in some sense malleable? In other words, is it capable of being molded and changed, so as to produce dramatic new thought patterns and life-changing habits?
- To just what extent can our brain power be amplified—especially in influencing the reactions and functions of our bodies?

- Is there a difference between the "mind" and the brain?
- Is there some connection between what we call the "spiritual" and the "mental" dimensions of our existence?
- What are the precise functions of different parts of the brain, and what can we do to enhance those functions?
- Will it ever be possible for the mind to reflect meaningfully, with a significant degree of understanding, on itself?

Many of these questions may never be answered completely. Some, however, *are* being answered, little by little, as we continue to investigate and push back the frontiers of psychophysiological research.

One of the major recent discoveries is that the brain is not a static, unchangeable entity. In fact, it's an organ capable of being transformed and utilized in new, remarkable ways. Through what I've called the Principle of Your Maximum Mind, the possibilities of this mental plasticity can be rather astounding, as the following cases demonstrate.

### *Return to the Himalayas*

Those of you who have read my previous books know that one of our research projects at the Harvard Medical School has been the exploration in the Indian Himalayas of the frontiers of the mind. This is the home in exile of the Dalai Lama and many Tibetan Buddhists. To be sure, other religions have also reported extraordinary physical and mental feats, healings and other dramatic events. But a number of years ago I decided to focus my efforts on investigating scientifically the claims of a particular Eastern tradition—Tibetan Buddhism.

One of the things that had interested me initially about these monks was their reported ability to raise their skin temperatures dramatically in cold environments through a form of meditation known as *gTum-mo* Yoga. This practice, which means literally "fierce woman," is supposed to create an internal fire of purification in the human body that counteracts falsehood and encourages a higher state of consciousness. As they meditate, the monks mentally follow an image of a bodily energy called "prana," which is supposed to ignite an intense "internal heat."

We were interested not only in the religious purpose of this practice but also in the physiological manifestations: If these monks could really raise their skin temperatures in cold situations, we knew we could measure the event with our instruments. The result, we expected, would be a deeper understanding of a mind-body interaction.

On our original trip to Upper Dharmsala in the foothills of the Indian Himalayas, our research team discovered that meditating monks, who were essentially unclothed, could in fact raise their skin temperatures by as much as 15 degrees Fahrenheit. Furthermore, they did this when the air temperature was only about 60 degrees. But more remained to be investigated in this area, more to be explored in the way the mind can influence the body.

Specifically, we had learned in 1978 through reading the works of Alexandra David-Neel that these monks could allegedly raise their skin temperatures high enough over sufficiently long periods of time to enable them to dry wet sheets on their bodies in wintry conditions. But up to that point, no scientists had succeeded in documenting the phenomenon. The reports were substantiated only by hearsay and legend. Our group of research scientists wished to investigate this fascinating story for ourselves.

In the summer of 1984, as part of our continuing collaboration, I received an invitation from the Dalai Lama to explore this phenomenon. I sent a filmmaking team to India to view and record the actual drying of the sheets—if indeed, the monks were able to achieve this feat. Our group, which included filmmakers Russell Pariseau and Michael Edwards, arrived at a Tibetan monastery in the Kulu Valley of northern India in February 1985. There the monks staged a secret ceremony, which, to the best of our knowledge, no other Westerners had ever before viewed.

With a growing sense of excitement, the filmmakers set up their equipment in the small monastery. They waited expectantly in a chilly room until about 3:00 A.M., when twelve monks entered. The indoor temperature there was just 40 degrees Fahrenheit. The monks proceeded to take off all their clothes except for small loincloths. The monks then assumed a cross-legged posture on the floor. They dipped cotton sheets, measuring three feet by six feet, into pails of water that had been placed in front of them; the water was about 49 degrees Fahrenheit.

Under the supervision of a monastic master, they then picked up the sopping wet sheets, wrung them out to get rid of the excess water, and then wrapped them around their upper bodies. The sheets were so wet that the cloths lay translucent against the monks' bodies: Their skin could be seen clearly through the wetness.

At this point the monks started to practice their *gTum-mo* Yoga meditation—and an amazing phenomenon began to occur. Although most people would have begun to shiver violently when exposed to such cold wetness, these monks didn't react at all. Instead, they sat calmly, and within three to five minutes, the sheets wrapped around them began to *steam*! The room filled with water vapor so that the lenses of the cameras became fogged over and had to be wiped off constantly. Within thirty to forty minutes, the sheets draped around the monks were completely dry.

Then the monks started all over again. They dipped another set of sheets into the cold water, wrung them out to some extent and draped these over their shoulders. As before, the monks began practicing their *gTum-mo* meditation. Again, the steaming started in three to five minutes, and the sheets were completely dry in another half hour or so. They then repeated the process once again. Although the entire ceremony took several hours, not once did the monks who were participating shiver or shake from the cold. Nor did they show any other signs of discomfort.

### *The Zero-Degree Experiment*

Our team next traveled to the Indian city of Leh, which is located on the western extension of the Tibetan plateau in Ladakh. The ultimate destination: a monastery nestled on a precarious precipice at 17,000 feet above sea level.

This is a high, arid plain punctuated by rocky pinnacles resembling gigantic geological spines, which jut upward toward the sky. The Hemis and Gotsang monasteries sit near the top of several of those spines at altitudes of approximately 17,000 feet. Observations were scheduled on a night Tibetans predicted would be one of the coldest of the year—February 5, 1985. In fact the temperature dropped to zero degrees Fahrenheit.

Dressed for near-Arctic climatic conditions, the filmmakers set out at midnight. They accompanied a group of ten monks, each clothed only in sandals, a loincloth and a light, cotton-type wrapping. The group eventually trekked to an even higher altitude—to a ledge over a sharp cliff at about 19,000 feet above sea level.

At this frigid, inhospitable spot, the monks took off their sandals and squatted down on their haunches. Then, they leaned forward, put their heads on the ground, and draped the light cotton wrappings over their bodies. In this position, being essentially naked, they spent the entire night practicing a special type of *gTum-mo* meditation called *Repeu*. It almost seemed that they had gone into some sort of suspended animation. They didn't even react as a light snow drifted down over them during the early morning hours.

No ordinary person could have endured these conditions. We're sure of that. Yet the monks showed no ill effects whatsoever. They simply remained quietly in their meditative positions for about eight consecutive hours. They were so still and silent that an uninitiated observer might have feared they had been frozen.

Finally, at the signal of the sounding of a small horn, they stood up, shook the snow off their backs, put their sandals on and calmly walked back down the mountain again. They might as easily have been a group of businessmen leaving their snug hotel rooms and heading for breakfast after a sound night's sleep.

There's no doubt that an ordinary person would have immediately gone into violent shivering during either the wet-sheets exercise or the zero-degree all-night outing. The body normally reacts this way just to generate enough heat to enable us to stay alive. In fact, without shivering or otherwise moving about, you or I would almost certainly have been unable to endure these challenges. Even with violent shivering in the zero-degree conditions, we would have developed frostbite and perhaps even died.

How could these monks achieve such feats?

I believe a key factor underlying any answer is their ability to elicit the Relaxation Response. As they engaged in a specific, profound prayer and meditation, relying firmly on their Buddhist faith, they experienced dramatic changes in their minds and bodies. But the Relaxation Response is just one of the physical and mental mechanisms at work in these monks. Although we don't have all the answers yet, some further explanations have been offered for their powers.

One leading theory is that the monks may have engaged in a process called nonshivering thermogenesis. This involves the ability of the body under some circumstances to burn or metabolize a type of fat called brown fat, which is able to generate very large amounts of heat. In the past, scientists thought that only certain types of nonhuman mammals, especially those which hibernate, could burn this type of fat. But now it appears that human beings may also have the capacity to generate heat from this fat. We hypothesize that the monks may have learned to do so through the use of generally unknown powers of the mind.

In any case, it's clear that our minds and bodies are capable of feats heretofore believed impossible—including, but certainly not restricted to, overcoming the effects of severe cold. But the dramatic possibilities are not just limited to Tibetan monks. They're open to you as well—as long as you learn how to tap your unused mental capacities.

### *The Secrets of the Sages*

The physical focal point of this power seems to be the special state which we identified more than a decade ago and called the Relaxation Response. I've already described the Relaxation Response briefly in the introductory chapter. How, exactly, do you elicit this response? What are the practical steps necessary to open the door to tremendous changes in the way we think and act?

There are several basic steps required to elicit the Relaxation Response.

**Step 1:** Pick a focus word or short phrase that's firmly rooted in your personal belief system. For example, a Christian person might choose the opening words of Psalm 23, "The Lord is my shepherd"; a Jewish person, "Shalom"; a nonreligious individual a neutral word like "one" or "peace."

**Step 2:** Sit quietly in a comfortable position.

**Step 3:** Close your eyes.

**Step 4:** Relax your muscles.

**Step 5:** Breathe slowly and naturally, and as you do, repeat your focus word or phrase as you exhale.

**Step 6:** Assume a passive attitude. Don't worry about how well you're doing. When other thoughts come to mind, simply say to yourself, "Oh, well," and gently return to the repetition.

**Step 7:** Continue for ten to twenty minutes.

**Step 8:** Practice the technique once or twice daily.

Our latest research has revealed that although all these steps are important, two are absolutely essential. These are the repetition of a word, sound, prayer, thought or muscular action and the passive attitude toward intruding thoughts. With these two conditions, you lessen the effects of distracting thoughts, activities and mechanisms which may prevent you from entering into a meditative state. Furthermore, the passive disregard of everyday thoughts helps you begin to break up some of the old negative thought patterns in your mind and opens you to positive, renewing influences which may be able to change your life.

By following these steps—if they are pursued in the context of your deepest beliefs—you will find that you're on the way toward expanding your mind's capabilities dramatically. You'll be moving in directions pioneered by the Tibetan monks, Christian and Jewish mystics and healers, and others whose lives are rooted in prayer and meditation. Also, as your mind expands to open the door to new inner adventures, you'll acquire a capacity to change personal habits—even those which weigh you down like the proverbial albatross. You'll increase your ability to develop positive new skills and disciplines.

*Your Marvelous Brain*

To get an idea how this capacity for change can be acquired, it's important to consider certain theories about the way the brain operates. But we must approach this subject with considerable humility. Although the results of brain research have dramatically expanded our knowledge in the last several decades, our understanding remains relatively rudimentary, given the incredible complexity of our brains.

Anatomically, the basic building block of the brain is the brain cell, or neuron. On one level, these cells may be viewed as living factories, which utilize blood-transported oxygen and sugar as fuel. This fuel, through well-defined biochemical steps, produces the energy that makes possible a vast number of biological tasks required to maintain the life of the cell. For example, each cell interacts with other cells, plays vital supporting roles in networks that produce thought and action, and, in the end, emits waste products which are carried off by the blood for elimination.

It's important to remember, though, that each of these brain cells is really *alive*, with all the potential for power and weakness that this condition entails. If the brain cell is deprived of its fuel—which comes primarily from the foods we eat and the air we breathe—it will die. In other words, if the blood supply, which carries this fuel to the brain, is blocked, as happens with severe hardening of the arteries, the brain and those cells supplied by the blocked artery can cease to function. A "stroke" or "shock" or cerebral vascular accident ensues

Among other things a healthy brain cell stores

and transmits information which ultimately becomes what we know as *thoughts*. It's very difficult to describe exactly what happens in this process because the whole act of thinking is so complex, with enormous numbers of brain cells interacting in our mental processes. Consider, for instance, that there are approximately 100 *billion* nerve cells in your brain.

Moreover, when you look closely at the makeup of each one of the 100 billion nerve cells, the whole matter gets indescribably more complicated. Each of the nerve cells has numerous tentacles, or axons and dendrites. During brain activity, these "communicate" with the tentacles of other cells through connections called synapses; thereby the brain cells interact and do their work. Dendrites also communicate with other parts of their own cell.

But now think of this: *Each* of the nerve cells has between 1,000 and 500,000 connections. And each brain cell connection has the potential to communicate with any other cell connection in the brain. This means the number of possible connections in the brain is incomprehensibly staggering.

How many connections are possible? Stated as a number, it's 25,000,000,000,000,000,000,000,000,000,000. Put another way, if you stacked upon your desk standard sheets of typing paper, one on top of the other, in an amount equal to the number of your possible brain connections, that stack would extend beyond the moon. It would extend beyond the planet Pluto. It would extend beyond our galaxy, and even well beyond the known limits of the entire universe, about 16 billion light years away!

With this incredible complexity, it's understandable that we may never be able to comprehend the full range of possibilities inherent in each of our brains. In fact, the more research that is done, the more awesome we discover the whole process of thought to be.

For example, we know now that these billions upon billions of connections in the brain "talk" to one another through certain chemicals in the brain. These chemicals, called neurotransmitters, are secreted at the tip of the connections of the brain cells. Thus, the connections between the brain cells are not physical connections Rather, there's a gap—a microscopic, minuscule gap—at each connection. The talking between one cell and another comes from the actions of those chemicals.

To make things even more involved, many of the nerve cells contain two or more neurotransmitter chemical agents, and more than sixty of these agents have been discovered to date. The complexity does not end there. As these brain chemicals reach across and communicate with other cells, they also influence other connections in their immediate environment. That is, they sort of "leak" around to other brain cell connections. These pervasive chemical actions are what allows a message to pass from one cell to others, and that's how we believe the talking between cells occurs.

There's still more. These messenger chemicals get into the bloodstream and may affect brain cells far away from their original source. Neurotransmitters actually produce changes in their own "home," or site of origin. They even influence their own production. Nor are the messages especially consistent. Each of the billions of nerve cells gives off different signals at different times, and is influenced by the signals received—the way they talk depends on the way they are talked to!

One of these neurotransmitters is an opium-like substance called endorphin. Endorphins may alleviate pain, produce euphoria under some circumstances, or they may act as a sedative. After endorphins are secreted by certain nerve cells of the brain, they may do their main work nearby, or they may take long trips to other, distant cells to produce feelings of well-being or relief from pain.

Some drugs have been developed which can mimic to one degree or another the operation of some of these neurotransmitters. Some will affect a person's mood or help treat patients beneficially in other ways. But the operation of drugs is extremely crude in comparison to the exquisite, highly tuned natural workings of the brain's neurotransmitters.

Other combinations of neurotransmitters are related to memory. One theory suggests that they give us the capacity for several types of memory: There is skill or procedural memory, which stores habits or "how-to" functions. There is declarative memory, which stores dates, numbers and other things you say after stating: "I remember. . . ." Thus in the two types of memory, you can remember how to ride a bicycle or hit a tennis ball, and you can remember what happened on your sixteenth birthday.

Your memories are derived in part from your life experiences themselves. They arise from the incredible capabilities of your brain, which allow your experiences to be received, encoded, stored, retrieved and interpreted. As we experience more, our brains store more and must therefore interpret more.

How do we sort out all of this information, so that when we are performing a specific task, we aren't overwhelmed and confused by all of our stored knowledge? How do we separate immediately meaningful, useful signals from all of the "noise" of memory?

Gradually, we're learning to reduce the complexity somewhat. In the process, we're finding we can understand a little better what's going on in our brains—and how we can use some of those awesome powers on a more practical basis. I've already referred briefly to one area of recent research—the so-called split-brain research—which is affording us an approach to understanding the workings of our brains and the possibilities for maximizing our minds.

Scientists working in that area have shown how the left hemisphere of the brain differs from and relates to the right—especially with patients who have suffered seizures, undergone brain surgery, or otherwise suffered neurological problems. In their studies, Drs. Sperry, Gazzaniga and others have discovered that the left and right hemispheres of the brain *tend* to have distinctive functions. And each set of functions is important to our fully integrated experience in the world as human beings.

For a right-handed person, the left hemisphere of the brain acts as a sort of "super press agent." It tries to make sense out of the huge quantities of new and stored information; the left side sifts and categorizes information. It makes inferences and predictions based on that information. To facilitate this inference-making function, the left hemisphere relies on vast reservoirs of analytical, logical and verbal skills. The fact that we can put thoughts in language and give precise reasons for why we do things is largely a direct result of this function of the left side of the brain.

The left side of the brain thus performs an invaluable service for us. We couldn't perform effectively as human beings without it. There's far too much information in our minds for us to be able to deal with it all, and the left side of the brain helps us, from moment to moment, select what's important to know.

Unfortunately, however, the left side is so important in this function that it has tended to overshadow the role of the right side of the brain. Yet the right side is a key to the plasticity of our minds, to our ability to change ingrained thought patterns and habits. It's a key to the operation of the Principle of Your Maximum Mind.

The right brain serves as a center of many of our intuitive, creative mental functions. Many times you'll have an insight or thought which seems to "come out of nowhere." You know it's a valid idea, but it didn't arrive through any logical, analytical process. Most likely, this idea or insight entered your mind through the actions of the neurotransmitters of the right hemisphere of the brain. Many of our artistic abilities and functions, including an ability to perceive things spatially, tend to be rooted in the right hemisphere. Then, after we receive this sort of input, the new information is transferred from the right side to the left for interpretation, selection and inference. Specifically, it passes through a connecting portion of the brain called the corpus callosum.

In effect, the operation of the left and right hemispheres of the brain are just one example of what Dr. Michael Gazzaniga has called "modules" in the brain. There are specific tasks that specific areas of the brain tend to handle more than other areas. One part specializes in mental images; another focuses on hearing functions; still another may deal primarily with feelings.

So what does all this have to do with your ability to change bad habits and develop new, constructive forms of self-discipline?

The problem we all face is that certain modules in the brain are so strong, and their patterns so deeply ingrained, that they tend to control others. In particular, this is a problem that seems to have developed many times in the relation between the left and right hemispheres. The left side of the brain—with its powerful abilities to analyze and make convincing inferences—may be portrayed in this context as a kind of "little dictator" over the right side. Many of our intuitive and creative functions, as well as much information that we need to know and use in changing our lives for the better, have in effect been enslaved by our rational left hemispheres. You might say we have become prisoners of the left sides of our brains.

So our goal can be characterized as a sort of inner, mental revolution: We must overthrow the hegemony of the left hemisphere and allow the right to break free and assume its full stature in the thinking process. In this way we can hope to open the door to beneficial change and growth in our lives.

But how much change can we expect from our brains—and what are the procedures through which it occurs?

# 3.

## *The Channels of Change*

The habits, thought patterns and attitudes that influence the way you think and behave are not etched in some gray concrete in your head. On the contrary, your mind and mine are malleable, capable of being molded into new shapes and forms, like some exquisite, living sculpture.

As we've seen, the left hemisphere of the brain—as essential and important as it is in helping us pursue meaningful, effective lives—tends to get in the way of our efforts to change ourselves. In a sense, the left brain may act as a kind of rigid intellectual guardian that thwarts any moves we make to change our habits and personal disciplines for the better.

It's not that the left hemisphere is inherently evil, or some sort of enemy which we need to engage in mortal combat. Rather, the left side has just been conditioned into thinking that certain things are good for us as human beings—when in fact those things may really be detrimental to our growth and well-being.

One example of how the left brain "guards" its domain can be found in a theory known in the psychological profession as cognitive dissonance. This is the concept, put forth by the pioneering social psychologist Dr. Leon Festinger, that when a belief and a behavior are in conflict, the belief must change to fit the behavior, or the behavior must change to conform to the belief. The left brain, upon confronting a belief-related conflict, is driven to make sense of it—to bring our values and actions into some sort of consistency. Usually, according to Festinger, it's the belief that does the changing.

One experiment which helped establish this conclusion involved students who were asked how they felt about cheating. Some of them said they felt it was a very bad thing, while others responded, in effect, "Gee, it's not really so bad, is it?"

Subsequently, all the students were given an examination in which it was very easy to cheat in a way that seemed undetectable. In fact the researchers *could* determine who was cheating and who wasn't. Those conducting the study found that even though many had initially said they thought cheating was bad, they did in fact cheat when given an easy opportunity. Then after the test was finished, all the students were again asked how they felt about cheating.

The results? Those who had initially felt cheating was bad but had actually engaged in cheating now said they felt cheating *wasn't* so bad. In other words, the students' values and actions ended up conforming more with one another when they were confronted with having to deal with this issue of cheating directly.

In this situation, the left brain stepped in and tried to make sense out of the difficult challenge facing these students. Through a process of rationalization, the students who cheated in violation of their anticheating beliefs found reasons to change their values. They seemed to decide that what they had done wasn't so bad. Furthermore, it would appear, they reasoned, "Everybody cheats in this sort of situation, so I may as well do the same. I may not be perfect, but I'm still a good person."

The value systems of some students fell captive to the need of the left brain to maintain logical consistency. This is just one instance of a much more pervasive problem. The left brain can imprison us with problems like phobias in much the same way.

Suppose, for example, you're standing in a supermarket line, with unpleasant crowds pushing in around you, and you develop a stomach pain. To make things worse, that stomach pain stays with you, and you become ill that evening.

It's quite possible that the left side of your brain, inferring a relationship between the pain and the supermarket line, may give you the message: "I shouldn't stand in supermarket lines—and if I do, the experience is going to be unpleasant." In fact this conclusion may be completely erroneous. There may be no relationship between your standing in the supermarket line and that stomach pain. But if your left-brain hemispheric activity somehow leads you to that conclusion, you could develop a fear of supermarket lines.

This obviously is a simplistic example and not one that's likely to happen to you in quite these terms. A more common experience is with airport crowds and lines. Some people hate to travel because they've had a series of unpleasant airport experiences which may have been exacerbated by other, unrelated problems that cropped up at those particular times. Soon these people begin to associate airports with unpleasant, anxiety-producing circumstances. As a result, they start to get anxious and uncomfortable even at the thought of heading for the airport.

Many phobias can develop this way. They may be the direct result of the interpretations and inferences that the left hemisphere gives to circumstances and feelings which we are experiencing.

Those confronted by such phobias, however, are not doomed to be enslaved forever by such fears. As we'll see in a subsequent chapter, many forms of psychotherapy and behavioral psychology have helped people change their brain patterns so that the phobias begin to fade and even disappear. One way which I've found to be successful in dealing with phobias is to get an individual to elicit the Relaxation Response regularly over a period of weeks and perhaps months. After this habit has become ingrained, it's much easier to correct the false interpretations that sustain the fear-producing situation and to deal with one's problems more constructively.

In other words, the brain really is capable of adaptation in overcoming many of these emotional shackles that bind us. But in physical terms, how does this occur?

### *How Mental Transformation Occurs*

In brief, the maximization of the mind may well work like this: When we change our patterns of thinking and acting, the brain cells begin to establish additional connections, or new "wirings." These new connections then communicate in fresh ways with other cells, and before long, the pathways or wirings that kept the phobia or other habit alive are replaced or altered.

As another example, if you decide you're going to learn to play tennis, you may take lessons and spend hour after hour on a court, practicing your strokes and honing your physical abilities. During this process, brain cells that control this particular skill establish new connections which enable you to play better than you could when you first started.

So it is with the thinking process. If you don't make any effort to change your way of thinking or develop new skills or disciplines, the brain cells will never establish the requisite new connections, or patterns. Similarly, if you don't work to maintain the new thought patterns and physical skills, they will diminish. It's clearly a case, as far as your brain is concerned, of "use it or lose it."

Aiding and underlying this process of change in the brain is the basic fact that the brain is a malleable, adaptable organ. The nervous system, including our mental powers, is not immutable. It's not unchangeable, with habits, thought patterns and skills permanently fixed. Thus, there is absolutely no reason you can't make considerable progress with all the self-help programs that have stymied you in the past. You really can achieve many of the improvements you've always wanted to see in your health, your spirituality and the other dimensions of your life. A key to this change is to learn to eliminate the unhealthy dictatorship of the left side of your brain and put both hemispheres of your brain in greater harmony.

The basic mechanism that enhances these processes of change is the Relaxation Response. It is the physiological door which will open the way for you to change your thought patterns and your life.

The Relaxation Response paves the way for beneficial brain change in a number of ways. First of all, measurements that we've done of those who are eliciting the Relaxation Response show that this phenomenon shuts off the distracting, stressful, anxiety-producing aspects of what is commonly called the "fight-or-flight response." With activation of the fight-or-flight reaction—when you get aroused, anxious or angry at a particular challenge or difficult situation—your body secretes certain hormones called catecholamines which "rev you up." They prepare you to deal quickly and decisively with a perceived threat.

In primitive situations, where dangers from wild animals might have been the order of the day, this sort of response was quite useful. In our own time, however, the fight-or-flight response tends to make us more nervous, uncomfortable and even unhealthy. Why? We don't utilize the physical outlets, like running or fighting, that were originally available to dissipate the energies from the enhanced hormonal changes that occur in our bodies. So we get tense and distracted, and our ability to achieve helpful change in our lives decreases or disappears completely.

As you might expect, the fight-or-flight response tends to be triggered by powerful and almost automatic inferences made by the left side of the brain: e.g., "tiger=run"; or "enemy=fight." But the Relaxation Response can help overcome these ingrained and now often inappropriate reactions, and it can shut off or prevent this type of improper arousal response. The Relaxation Response does not significantly alter arousal when a true danger or demanding situation is present. In a major crisis, hazardous and demanding circumstances overpower the Relaxation Response effects, perhaps because survival is at stake.

The Relaxation Response can also encourage important brain activity which increases communication between the left and right hemispheres of the brain. Scientific studies have confirmed that during the elicitation of the Relaxation Response, the two sides of the brain begin to interact more, as evidenced by similar brain-wave patterns occurring simultaneously in the left and right hemispheres. Researchers, in doing electroencephalograms of individuals who are in the process of eliciting the Relaxation Response, have discovered that there is increased coherence of the so-called alpha and theta brain-wave frequencies between the left and right sides of the brain at those times.

Most important of all, this mental state sets the stage for significant change. Among other things, it's apparently easier to think creatively when your brain is operating with the left and right sides more in synchrony. You can more easily examine and use the information taken in both by the left and right sides of the brain, without the interference of extraneous thoughts, which may get in the way under other circumstances. So when you're in this state of enhanced left-right hemispheric communication, it's easier to process information and view situations in a new and innovative way. In other words, a "cognitive receptivity" or "plasticity of cognition" occurs, in which you actually change the way you view the world.

This plasticity is utilized in the process of hypnosis. Our research has shown that to pass into the so-called hypnotic state, the Relaxation Response is first elicited. Then, the hypnotist may suggest various actions to the individual being hypnotized. These may include suggestions for remembering otherwise forgotten events or for performing certain movements, such as the levitation of an arm.

It's interesting that many people who have elicited the Relaxation Response—and experienced increased communication between the two sides of the brain—express the experience as a sort of "wholeness." They use such terms as "unboundedness," "infinite correlation," "well-being," and "intense wakefulness." Also, those in this state tend to have much greater awareness of the richness of details which surround them in their environment.

Often people just say that the state is inexpressible; it's beyond words and language and can only be felt, not described. In its most intense form, this type of experience is known as a "peak experience"—whether you're talking about a spiritual insight, a winning sports effort or some personal intellectual breakthrough.

Dr. Stanley R. Dean, professor of psychiatry at the

Universities of Miami and Florida, discusses this type of peak experience as one that "produces a superhuman transmutation of consciousness that defies description. The mind, divinely intoxicated, literally reels and trips over itself, groping and struggling for words of sufficient exaltation and grandeur to portray the transcendental vision. As yet, we have no adequate words."

Dean then cites a portion of a poem by T. S. Eliot in *Four Quartets* as appropriate, even though used by Eliot in another context:

> . . . Words strain,
> Crack and sometimes break under the burden,
> Under the tension, slip, slide, perish,
> Decay with imprecision, will not stay in place,
> Will not stay still. . . .

Of course no one has peak experiences on a consistent basis. In fact, many people never reach the mental or spiritual mountaintops that others can achieve. But no matter how far you're able to go, there's no question you'll be better able to improve your life—if you can just learn to increase the coherence of the left and right sides of the brain through the use of the Relaxation Response.

### *The Faith Factor*

Another major factor in enabling you to change your brain and your life—one which I've briefly alluded to before—is the intensity of your personal belief system.

The brain responds and changes when deep personal belief and conviction take hold in our lives. Our beliefs and convictions are part of our thoughts and thus part of our brains. When we think or act out of a deep conviction, we are tapping into an already existing "brain wiring." As a result, we feel that what we're doing is true and correct; we feel comfortable operating on a foundation of deeply held convictions.

Under these circumstances, new thought patterns and actions can develop much more readily. The "tracks" are, if you will, already "greased" and the new patterns more easily established. The neurotransmitters in the cells may thus transmit new messages more easily, and this, in turn, facilitates the development of the newer thought processes, skills and disciplines.

While many factors contribute to the development of these new pathways, grooves and wiring configurations in the brain, belief often remains a primary driving and enhancing force. A good illustration of the power of belief in mind-body interactions in medical research involves what is known as the placebo effect.

This phenomenon, which I've described in both *The Mind/Body Effect* and *Beyond the Relaxation Response,* has three essential components: beliefs and expectations on the part of a patient or person being healed; beliefs and expectations of the doctor, health professional or healer; and beliefs and expectations inherent in the relationship of health professional to patient or healer to patient.

To explore the power of the patient's belief, researchers studied one group of women who were suffering from nausea and vomiting during pregnancy. First, the women were asked to swallow small, intragastric balloons, which measured their stomach contractions. The balloons detected characteristic waves of nausea and vomiting. Then, they were given a substance which they were told would cure their vomiting and nausea. In fact, however, they were given syrup of ipecac, a medication often used to *cause* vomiting.

The results? In this case, belief triumphed over physical forces and medicine. Because they believed they were getting antinausea medication, for many of the women nausea and vomiting disappeared and, as measured in the balloon, their stomach contractions also returned to normal. Here we have a situation where the belief in a substance actually reversed the physiological action of the drug. The wiring of the brain was more powerful than the drug.

A related but more negative example of the power of individual belief on one's brain involves one type of sudden death—fatalities among crime victims. Sometimes, acute fear or terror induced by belief can release very large amounts of a stress-related hormone, norepinephrine, which can have devastating physical effects. The release of too much of this substance may trigger a series of biochemical steps which ends in massive changes in the heart muscle—and death. One scientific study showed that eleven of fifteen subjects who were victims of physical assault and died as a result of the attacks did not sustain any internal injuries, according to the autopsies. Instead, they had suffered a condition known as myofibrillar degeneration, or a type of heart muscle damage.

This could be the same process by which voodoo death occurs in certain primitive societies. There, a curse may be pronounced on an individual by a powerful medicine man. The victim often dies quickly afterward.

It's his *belief* that he's going to die that kills him, more than anything else. Similarly, the people who died during mugging attacks expired from the results of their belief in the possible harm from the attack, rather than from the attack itself.

Other studies have shown that the belief of the physician or healer is also extremely important. One group of physicians working in conjunction with a drug company was given the same generic tranquilizer, but under two different brand names, only one of which was from their company. They were then asked to test the two brands.

The results showed that the substance which was labeled as being produced by their own company did better than the other brand, even though there was no difference between the two substances except their names. In short, it was the belief of the physicians in their own product which seemed to make the difference in the way the product worked on patients.

An example of the third element in the placebo effect—the power of the doctor-patient relationship—involves a study that was conducted at Massachusetts General Hospital with two similar groups of patients who were about to undergo surgery. They were approached by an anesthetist in two different ways. He dealt with one group of patients in a rather cursory fashion. With the other group the same anesthetist behaved in a much warmer, more sympathetic fashion. He sat down on the bed, explained in detail what was going to occur in the operation, described the amount and type of pain to be expected, and, in general, was extremely supportive. He established a solid doctor-patient relationship, and as a result, the patients developed confidence and positive belief or faith in the physician.

Then all the patients went through their surgery and postsurgical procedures. All were allowed to receive as much pain-alleviating medication as they requested. During this phase, all were treated by hospital personnel who either did not know to which group the patients belonged or who were unaware the test was being conducted.

After the study was completed, the investigators found that the patients who had been treated in a warm and sympathetic manner asked for half as much pain-killing medication as the other group. Also, the ones who had enjoyed the warm doctor-patient relationship were discharged from the hospital on average 2.7 days sooner than the other group.

In each of these situations, the power of belief on healing is evident. The mind begins to work independently of medication and other factors and in effect takes on a life of its own in influencing bodily reactions. In short, beliefs seem capable of enhancing and transforming the mind with dramatic results.

### *What Are the Limits of Change?*

What ultimate limits are possible as you attempt to change your thought patterns and your life?

Great change is indeed possible for each individual. But if you want to become a musician at age forty, the chances are you won't be able to turn yourself into a modern-day Mozart or Beethoven. If you want to learn how to play tennis, you probably can't hope to compete with the likes of Ivan Lendl or Martina Nav-

| ME | | | MOZART |
|---|---|---|---|
| BEFORE | AFTER | BEFORE | AFTER |
| LITTLE | | | MUCH |

**MUSICAL ABILITY**

ratilova. It's necessary to begin developing some skills at an early age if you hope to achieve your peak. Even if you do begin at an early age, there are genetic limits on how far you can go.

To understand just what your genetic limits in changing your brain may be, it's helpful to think in terms of a horizontal line for each area of behavior or thought that you hope to transform.

Suppose, for example, you want to develop your musical ability even though you've already reached middle age. On the left side of the line, you might write the words "Me—Before," to indicate where you stand in ability before you begin to learn the new skill. On the far right-hand side of the line, you might write "Mozart." Then, somewhere in the middle area, you might write "Me—after five years of hard work and study."

In other words, you definitely have the potential to improve your natural ability after a certain amount of work and discipline. But no matter how hard you work at this point in your life, you'll probably never reach the regions on that line near Mozart's achievements—he simply began with great gifts. On the other hand, there is hope that if you get in the right frame of mind and rely on the Principle of Your Maximum Mind, you will enhance the probabilities of achieving a great deal—regardless of your age and native abilities.

• • •

One of the most puzzling and mysterious issues that faces those doing brain research is the distinction between the *mind* and the *brain*. Is the mind the same as the brain? Or is the mind somehow made up of features which transcend the physical makeup of the brain?

There's been considerable discussion about this point over the years. Some argue that our minds are the sum total of our brain's physical capabilities, nothing more and nothing less. But Sir John Eccles, who won the Nobel Prize for Medicine in 1963, has rejected such a mechanistic view of man's thinking processes. He doesn't think that the power of the mind rests exclusively in nerve cells, dendrites, synapses and neurotransmitters.

Rather, he states, "I believe that there is a fundamental mystery in my existence, transcending any biological account of the development of my body (including my brain) with its genetic inheritance and its evolutionary origin."

Eccles goes on to argue, "If I say that the uniqueness of the human self is not derived from the genetic code, nor derived from experience, then what is it derived from? My answer is this: from a divine creation. Each self is a divine creation."

In a similar vein, the famous Canadian neurosurgeon Wilder Penfield wrote in *The Mystery of the Mind* that the workings of the mind will probably always be impossible to explain simply on the basis of electrical or chemical action in the brain and nervous system.

"The mind is independent of the brain," he declared. "The brain is a computer, but it is programmed by something that is outside itself, the mind."

Roger Sperry, the Nobel Prize winner who has done so much of the significant split-brain research, doesn't go quite as far as either Eccles or Penfield. But he does conclude that the mind is "the crowning achievement of some five hundred million years or more of evolution." He also suggests that the mind somehow is more than the sum of the physical mechanisms and components of the brain. In other words, just as hydrogen and oxygen combine to produce water, which is quite different from the component parts, so the parts of the brain combine to produce a mind which transcends its purely molecular foundations.

Is it possible to define the "mind"?

In scientific terms, we simply can't be definitive. The mind certainly resides in large part in the brain; in many ways, it also seems to go beyond individual brain components. Religious groups have long recognized this transcendent feature of our consciousness, as they use terms like the human spirit or similar metaphysical language. There is a link between religious insight and this phenomenon of the mind, which somehow seems to transcend the physical. In this regard, it's interesting to me that the Relaxation Response, with all its physiological benefits, has most often and effectively been elicited through forms of prayer.

Clearly, we've now moved to some of the outer edges of scientific thought and understanding. Even though there's a great deal we don't know, and may never know, about the workings of the brain and the mind, I believe we have sufficient justification to recognize, and try to make use of, the phenomenon which I have called the Principle of the Maximum Mind—an ability of human beings to break through ingrained habits and thought patterns and transform their lives. The fundamental features of this principle, as we've seen, include:

- The capacity to overcome the "dictatorship" of the left side of the brain, and increase communication and coherence between the left and right hemispheres;
- The plasticity of the brain, or its ability to be molded and shaped through the transformation of cells and the establishment of new pathways;
- A central role of belief in triggering important changes in the brain and mind; and
- A pivotal role of the Relaxation Response in helping to open the door to life-changing transformations.

Now, with these basics in mind, let's consider some practical ways that you can use the Principle of the Maximum Mind to change your life.

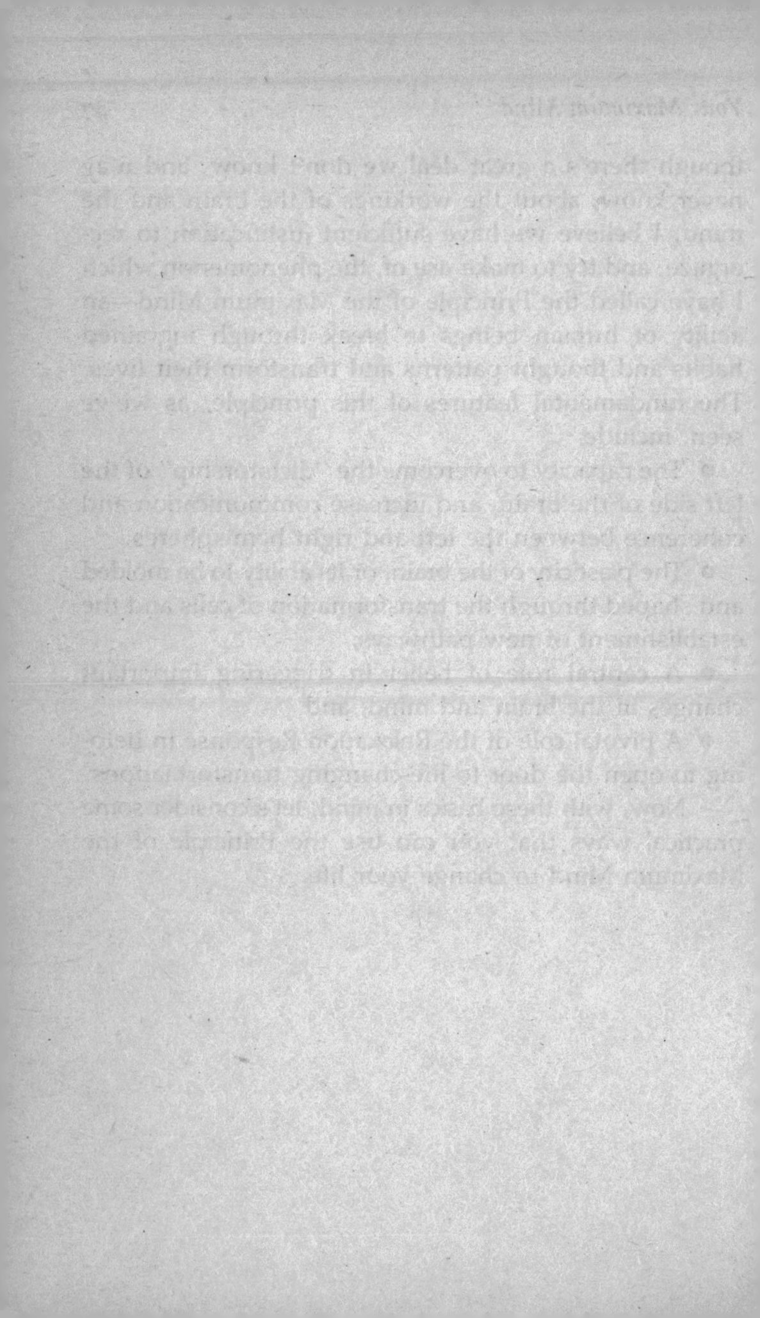



though there's a great deal we don't know, and may never know, about the workings of the brain and the mind, I believe we have sufficient information to begin—and try to make use of the phenomenon which I have called the Principle of the Maximum Mind—an ability of human beings to break through ingrained habits and thought patterns and transform their lives. The fundamental features of this principle, as we've seen, include:

- The capacity to overcome the "dictatorship" of the left side of the brain and increase communication and coherence between the left and right hemispheres;
- The plasticity of the brain, or its ability to be molded and shaped through the transformation of cells and the establishment of new pathways;
- A critical role for belief in achieving important changes in the brain and mind; and
- A pivotal role of the Relaxation Response in helping to open the door to life-changing transformations.

Now, with these basics in mind, let's explore some practical ways that you can use the Principle of the Maximum Mind to change your life.

# PART II

• • •

# *How to Change Your Life*

# The Ultimate Self-Help System

We live in what might be called the "Self-Help Society": Many of us focus primarily on certain personal problems we have, and we're constantly seeking ways to overcome those problems. We become enamored of practical techniques and programs—many of which we find presented as step-by-step guidelines or principles in various popular magazines and books. There are in fact so many self-help books that they now require a separate section in bookstores.

Basically, there's nothing wrong with this emphasis on trying to improve oneself. In fact, if more of us were concerned about eliminating our faults and bad habits and developing constructive new disciplines, this world might be a better place altogether.

But why are self-improvement programs often unsuccessful? The answer may lie in at least two major problems that may develop with any self-help program. On the one hand, we may lack the discipline to stick with a self-help regimen and experience any change in our lives at all. On the other, life-transforming efforts that get out of control and become obsessive may do us more harm than good. In fact, as we'll see in a later chapter, opening yourself to significant change through unsupervised meditation may actually be dangerous.

### *Some Basic Rules for Self-Improvement*

To assist you in beginning a safe and effective approach to self-improvement, let me suggest three basic rules to follow. These will maximize your efforts to change yourself for the better because they'll help you to incorporate the Principle of the Maximum Mind in your life.

**Rule #1: Don't try to substitute self-help efforts for a basic belief system.** There may be a problem with following self-help programs if they are merely a substitute for an authentic search for a deeper meaning of life. Many times people pursue a personal improvement program in a conscious or subconscious effort to find a satisfying, comprehensive world view. There may even be an implied desire to cheat death and become immortal.

A person who starts out by wanting to get in good physical condition may end up becoming a physical fitness addict whose waking hours are consumed with exercise, diet and fitness reading. I've known people—and I'm sure you have, too—who have become so obsessed with fitness that other important concerns and responsibilities, such as their family involvement, get neglected. Some marathon runners, for example, develop a chronic family condition known as the "marathon-widow syndrome." In this situation, the spouse is left alone at home while his or her mate is on long conditioning runs or participating in races. When a self-help regimen gets out of control in this way there can be dire results.

I know of a case where a professional man—whom we'll call Bill—became so obsessed with lowering his marathon times that he spent two or more hours in training at the end of each day. Bill was married and the father of three children. He found he didn't have sufficient time to spend with his family—at least not if he hoped to continue his exercise program.

If you're not a runner or amateur athlete, you may wonder, "What on earth was this guy thinking of—to forget his family life and spend all his time pounding the pavement?" But if you've ever done any distance running, you'll probably understand some of the attraction.

In part, the appeal of this type of sport involves the elicitation of the Relaxation Response. As a distance runner's feet hit the pavement in a rhythmic pattern, the physiological effects of the Relaxation Response occur, and the mind becomes more open to change. This state can be a very pleasurable and peaceful phenomenon. That's why well-conditioned runners, after they've been doing road work for at least fifteen or twenty consecutive minutes, often feel they could go on forever. In fact, many report an experience which has been called the "runner's high."

With Bill, our marathon runner, the pleasurable

sensations and the mental openness to higher levels of physical conditioning apparently resulted in a life-changing experience. Bill had been quite unathletic in his younger life, and he had felt inadequate when in the company of his more sports-oriented colleagues. He often wished that he could get into good physical condition and do well in physical activities. But he never seemed to have either the motivation or the natural athletic ability to embark successfully on a training program.

When he discovered marathon running, however, he had finally found his niche. After he had spent a few weeks developing a basic level of conditioning, he really *wanted* to continue with the program. In other words, after he had taken an initial step toward changing his life, the regular elicitation of the Relaxation Response in the repetitive act of distance running had opened him up to further change.

Almost before he knew what was happening, his entire life had been transformed. He had reordered his priorities and his time commitments so that he could carry out two hours or more of running each day. In addition, he often devoted entire weekends to traveling out of town so that he could participate in marathon events. In effect, his running became his life. Everything else took second place—including his marriage and family.

In Bill's case, his wife eventually divorced him. At first he was distraught and he couldn't understand what had happened. As he thought back on the situation, he recalled that his wife and his children had complained and pleaded with him to spend less time running and more time with them. Somehow, though, he had assumed that they weren't really as upset as they sometimes seemed to be. Besides, he was so excited about the change that he saw occurring in his body and his life that he found he simply couldn't stop what was really his destructive behavior.

Clearly, Bill had plunged into a self-help program without considering all the consequences. He had failed to evaluate how his physical conditioning and marathon-running commitment should fit into all aspects of his life.

Bill didn't have any particular religious beliefs but he did affirm the importance of certain family values. As he thought back over his broken marriage, he acknowledged that if he had it to do over again, he would try to promote a stable and happy family life more than his middle-aged athletic aspirations. To be sure, his marathon running was extremely important to him and had given him a new sense of self-worth and personal confidence. But he let this avocation get out of hand. He moved ahead with an all-too-consuming self-improvement program which left little time or energy for his other important commitments.

Bill waited too late to do anything about saving his family life. You can learn from his mistakes. It's a matter first of deciding what your basic beliefs in life are. Then, you should make any self-help effort conform to those beliefs. If your self-improvement program becomes the be-all and end-all—the source of your basic understanding of life—you may very well find your life changing for the worse. But if a self-help effort is properly integrated into a broader belief system, you'll likely find your life much more rewarding.

**Rule #2: Rely on a maximum mind guide.** In my

previous writing, I've emphasized the importance of eliciting the Relaxation Response in the context of a tried-and-true religious faith and tradition for those who believe in God. As such a person moves more deeply into life-changing, maximum mind programs, I believe the reliance on traditional religion becomes even more important.

In particular, it's advisable for a religiously inclined person not only to rely in general on an established religious faith, but also to rely on a specific spiritual guide in that faith. If you're not particularly religious, you should find what I'd call a "maximum mind guide"—a mature person who can help you keep your basic value system in perspective as you begin to change through the powerful Principle of the Maximum Mind.

Who exactly should be your spiritual or maximum mind guide?

If your program is related to the correction of a health problem, the aid of a qualified, understanding and knowledgeable health professional is advisable. If you wish to give more emphasis to spirituality, there are those in every major religion who have advanced far enough in spiritual growth and techniques to be able to advise and guide those who are newcomers. The guide, in this case, could be your pastor, your priest or your rabbi. The person you choose should be not just a nominal member of that particular tradition. Rather, the person should be steeped and well versed in the spiritual subtleties of your particular belief system.

A spiritual or maximum mind guide becomes especially important as you devote more of your time and energy to potentially potent self-improvement programs that you expect to change your life. You need someone to help you get perspective on how your attempts to transform yourself are fitting into your fundamental value system.

For example, are you going too far, like the marathon runner in the previous example? Or are you not going far enough? Is your self-improvement program enhancing other aspects of your life? Or is it detracting from important relationships and activities? What's the ultimate goal of the program?

If you don't answer this last question adequately, you may find yourself devoting months or even years to going in a direction that is actually unproductive. One woman was trying to decide whether to develop her bridge-playing skills or devote extra time to helping the homeless. She chose the card-playing option, and certainly, she enjoyed it greatly. In fact, she did rather well in several tournaments.

But after about three years of this sort of activity, she looked back on her life and decided, quite sadly, that she had, indeed, changed her life and improved her abilities—in the wrong direction. Given her personal value system, she would have felt much more satisfied in the end if she had given the goal of helping others more of a priority. A proper maximum mind or spiritual guide could have helped her make the right decision at the very beginning.

An appropriate guide, though, should not be some sort of all-knowing guru or mini-ruler who gives you a blueprint for action that you must follow without question. The most helpful guides are *question askers* who point out issues you may have overlooked. They are at their best when they encourage you to think again about values which you may have temporarily overlooked.

**Rule #3: Begin any attempt to change your life with a positive attitude.** With most people, the main problem is not the self-help program that gets out of control. Rather, it's an inability to get moving at all. Most of us simply don't seem to have the discipline even to get started on a self-help program. We say we want to learn that foreign language, become proficient on the guitar, lose twenty pounds, get into good physical condition, or develop a more solid spiritual life. But after a series of false starts, we finally give up. We decide that we just don't have the inner fortitude or "get up and go" to change our lives.

Because of past patterns of failure, we may develop negative attitudes about ourselves and our ability to change. We decide that an inability to do something reflects "just the way we are," and we stop trying. In fact change may still be possible: It's just a matter first of finding the door through which beneficial improvement can enter and then simply learning how to open it.

For most people the first step in embarking on a successful self-improvement program is to get rid of the doubts and negative feelings about themselves and their potential. No matter how often you fail at something, there's still a possibility that you can succeed. It's first and foremost a matter of *believing* that progress or development is possible.

This "can-do" attitude is often tagged as "positive thinking." Unfortunately, the very popularization of these concepts through the writings of Norman Vincent Peale and others has made them so familiar that we may dismiss them too readily, or perhaps think we understand more than we actually do.

When Peale's book *The Power of Positive Thinking* was published in the 1950s, the impact was immediate and dramatic. Despite the seeming newness of the ideas, there was extensive precedent for the upbeat gospel presented in this volume. Peale was continuing a tradition with American roots extending back to the Transcendentalism of Ralph Waldo Emerson, to the New Thought movement of the mid-nineteenth century, and also to an upbeat Christian philosophy of life. Millions responded to Peale's books and sermons because they knew, perhaps intuitively, that he had articulated a concept which was fundamental to success, satisfaction and happiness in life. Reverend Robert H. Schuller, with his concept of "possibility thinking," and other later writers and speakers have continued to emphasize the main points popularized by Peale.

### *Positive Thinking: The Centerpiece of Self-Improvement*

In many ways, the positive-thinking attitude is the *sine qua non* of any successful self-improvement effort. In other words, you must *think* you can achieve a self-help goal before you can expect to reach that goal.

Why should this be?

There are a number of reasons positive thinkers prevail over negative thinkers. For one thing, if you think you can do something, you're more likely to attempt it and then keep on trying until you have given your goal a decent try. Of course sometimes you may very well be wrong. You may try several things and fail. But at least the *possibility* is there that you'll be able to achieve something worthwhile. Conversely, if you think you can't do something, you're likely not to try at all. Or you may try so halfheartedly that you give up at the first sign of difficulty.

Also, a person who's a positive thinker tends to be more alert to opportunities. If you think negatively, you'll often overlook the subtle possibilities of different situations. A life-changing opportunity may be staring you right in the face, and you won't be able to see it because, in effect, your vision is obstructed by negative blinders.

In this regard, I'm reminded of one sage in the American Evangelical movement who was having great difficulty finding time to pursue his prayer life. He simply couldn't seem to get up in the mornings early enough to put in the time he felt his devotions warranted. During the main part of the day, he was too busy with his work and teaching responsibilities. And in the evening, most of his time was committed to his family. In short, every avenue for pursuing this particular form of spiritual discipline appeared to be blocked.

This man was a positive thinker—and he was determined to do something about his prayer life. He knew he couldn't reach the levels of spiritual growth that he wanted without prayer. So he kept looking. Finally, he noticed that later in the evenings, between about nine-thirty and ten-thirty, there was a lull in his family activities. His children were either asleep or deeply involved in their own projects; his wife was usually off doing something by herself at this time. So he found that he could go back to his room and enjoy at least an hour of uninterrupted quiet to pursue his prayers.

The main thing that enabled this man to find the

answer to his problem was an attitude of positive expectation. He wouldn't allow a negative approach to blind him to the possibilities of change in his life.

### *How Gail Became More Positive*

How do you become positive—especially if much of your time seems to be spent dwelling on negatives? Or to use the terms that we've employed so far in this book, how can you start to "rewire" your brain connections so that positive thinking becomes easier and more automatic?

One businesswoman named Gail faced some incredibly rough times several years ago. She lost her job, went through a divorce and lost her mother and younger brother in a fatal car accident. Gail had always tended to be a person who saw the negative side of things, rather than the positive. This series of misfortunes made her even more of a pessimist.

Gail's naturally negative predispositions combined with the series of personal crises to produce a negative cycle of thinking from which she seemed unable to escape. By repetitive use of negative thought patterns these pathways or wirings in her brain became relatively "fixed" in unproductive directions. The left hemisphere of her brain began to make an overabundance of unhelpful inferences about the lack of possibilities in her life. She simply couldn't seem to break free of this mindset.

As you might expect, this negative way of thinking manifested itself in a number of ways, both emotional and physical. Gail began to believe that she was an unworthy person, and as a result, she had a great deal of trouble getting a good job. On the few occasions when she was hired, she lasted in the position only a few months before she was fired. The problem wasn't her abilities. Rather, Gail started *expecting* to be fired, and before long, her attitudes resulted in self-fulfilling prophecies.

In addition, her personal relationships suffered. She withdrew more and more into herself and steadily cut off her connections with her friends. It wasn't that her friends and loved ones wanted to break off contact. Rather, Gail herself lost interest in others and felt that she had very little to offer them. She was embarrassed by her failures in life and simply didn't want to have to confront other people who reminded her of the happier life she had once led.

She also developed a number of bodily ailments. At first, it was a general malaise, a sense of not feeling well in the mornings or suffering from vague aches and pains later in the day. Later the situation became worse. She developed a chronic back problem, and her doctors couldn't locate any source of the pain and discomfort.

In all, Gail's life seemed to be moving on an irreversible downward course. It seemed that nothing she or anyone else could do or say would bring her back to an even keel in her personal life and relationships.

One thing Gail had managed to hold on to during these bad times was the seed of a faith planted in her early in childhood. Although she withdrew from the company of people who might have been able to encourage her and build her up, the isolation may have been what finally helped her.

As she spent long hours alone, she began to rely

more and more on prayer. In the past, when her life had been filled with family and work concerns, she had given little time to prayer or meditation. She simply didn't have time. Now, with nowhere else to turn but her religion, she began to spend long periods, sometimes an hour or more, in prayer and meditation. Occasionally the prayers and thoughts she would offer up to God were as negative as the rest of her attitudes. But more and more she began to enjoy this time of spiritual communication.

Certainly Gail's spiritual life was developing in more productive directions during this period. At the same time, important changes were evidently taking place in her brain. As we've seen, periods of meditation which last for ten to twenty minutes or longer will change the way the left and right hemispheres of the brain communicate with one another. Moreover, this increased coherence of the right and left hemispheres of the brain tends to open a person up to change. It appears we are better able to process new information at that time.

In Gail's case, the increased openness could have gone either way, depending on what sorts of influences she exposed herself to immediately following the times of meditation. If she had dwelt on how terrible her life was, the negative pathways in her brain would have become more and more fixed.

Gail took a more edifying approach. She happened to pick up a self-help, positive-thinking book one day when she was browsing through a bookstore. Rather significantly, perhaps, Gail was not much of a reader. So this book was practically the only book that she had in her home. The only other thing that she read on a regular basis was her Bible.

As a result, Gail exposed her mind to this little self-help volume more than any other book, magazine or newspaper during large portions of the day. She found several sections of it so inspiring that she tended to stare at them and read them over and over again.

Without being at all aware of what she was doing, Gail thus began to reprogram her way of thinking along more positive and productive lines. As she alternated between her prayers, the self-help book and the Bible, she soon found that her outlook on life brightened considerably. Then, one of those once-in-a-lifetime experiences occurred: As she was sitting in an easy chair musing after a period of prayer and inspirational reading, she had what can only be described as a kind of religious conversion.

Gail had the distinct feeling, a feeling which quickly turned into a solid conviction, that her life could be turned around. Along with this feeling, she had an overwhelming sense of God's presence with her. She no longer felt alone. She found herself wanting, for the first time in months, to go out and reestablish old friendships, make new ones, and try to get her career moving again.

She immediately started including notes in her daily diary about calls she needed to make and plans for a job search she wanted to put into effect. Then she noticed another dramatic thing: Her back was no longer painful. She pressed her spine in several places which had been tender, but nothing bothered her. At her next appointment with the doctor, she was told that her back ailment had apparently been alleviated.

Gail's full emotional recovery did take considerable time. It was several months before she was able to get back into the job market, and it also took time to re-establish various personal contacts. Some people couldn't believe that such a dramatic change had taken place in her personality. She seemed like the "old" Gail they had known before. In any event, there was no question that something significant had happened in her life when she had been deeply involved in prayer and meditation in her living room.

### *The Mechanism of Change*

What exactly was the source of the change? As with many life-changing experiences that are rooted in a religious faith, the spiritual element, as mysterious and inexplicable as it may be, has to be taken seriously. This woman's growing belief that her life could be changed, along with whatever outside or inside force that inspired and sustained that belief, was obviously a major factor.

On the other hand, it's fairly obvious to me that certain physiological changes were taking place simultaneously in Gail. Through the operation of the Principle of the Maximum Mind, new pathways developed in her brain which altered her thought processes and behavior patterns for the better. In other words, she first elicited the Relaxation Response through prayer. Then, having become open to change in this way, she exposed herself, perhaps accidentally, to information and influences which would effect a beneficial transformation.

The powerful combination of these mental and spiritual forces apparently brought about a healing of her emotions and her back problems which had seemed intractable to other remedies. I expect that if her efforts to renew her mind and spirit had taken place under the guidance of an appropriate spiritual guide or a physician who understood these principles, she might have undergone this change in her life even more quickly.

In many ways Gail's experience—though she was quite unaware of what was happeninig—stands as a prototype of how a person can open an inner doorway to a life-transforming experience. If we want to change ourselves, we must first open up our minds to the forces of renewal. That means using techniques of meditation or prayer rooted in our deepest beliefs. Then we must expose ourselves to influences which are going to move us in the direction of change that we have chosen.

For many people, an essential initial step for moving into this life-transforming attitude is to develop a positive, can-do approach to life. In other words, before you embark on any self-help program—whether to improve your physical condition, alleviate your physical ailments, acquire new learning, enhance your creativity or enrich your spiritual life—it's a good idea to become convinced that *you really can do it*. And that means becoming more positive in your thinking.

To this end, I want to encourage you to try a positive-thinking exercise which should be the first practical thing you do to change your way of thinking and acting. First, discuss your course of action with your maximum mind guide. Then, move on to the two phases of the exercise, which are the prerequisites for incorporating the Principle of the Maximum Mind in your life.

First, you "open the door" of your mind to change by eliciting the Relaxation Response.

Then, immediately expose yourself to information or other influences which will help "reprogram" or "rewire" your mind along more productive lines.

Now set aside twenty to thirty minutes and prepare to turn yourself into a more positive person. First, elicit the Relaxation Response.

**Step 1:** Pick a focus word or short phrase that's firmly rooted in your personal belief system. A Christian person might choose the opening words of Psalm 23, "The Lord is my shepherd"; a Jewish person, "Shalom"; a nonreligious individual a neutral word like "one" or "peace."

**Step 2:** Sit quietly in a comfortable position.

**Step 3:** Close your eyes.

**Step 4:** Relax your muscles.

**Step 5:** Breathe slowly and naturally and, as you do, repeat your focus word or phrase as you exhale.

**Step 6:** Assume a passive attitude. Don't worry about how well you're doing. When other thoughts come to mind, simply say to yourself, "Oh, well," and gently return to the repetition.

**Step 7:** Continue for ten to twenty minutes.

**Step 8:** Practice the technique once or twice daily.

Immediately after you've spent ten to twenty minutes eliciting the Relaxation Response, you're ready to move into the second phase of the Principle of the Maximum Mind. Begin to focus your thinking on some positive concept, passage of writing or even something visual. For example, you might find a happy, upbeat picture, such as a child smiling. Then, study that picture for five or ten minutes. See every element of happiness and joy that you can possibly find in it. Or if you choose a written passage, it will be helpful to concentrate on something that is rooted in your personal belief system, such as a passage of Scripture or a personally meaningful poem.

Before you get started on this life-changing approach to prayer and meditation, it's important to make a key distinction between the two phases or stages of the Principle of the Maximum Mind, between the meditation and prayer which elicits the Relaxation Response and the focused thinking which helps to fix the new direction that you want your life to take.

In the first phase, the elicitation of the Relaxation Response comes through open-ended and undirected prayers and meditations. You're *not supposed to concentrate* on trying to change yourself. In fact, if you do try to concentrate, you'll lose the passive attitude that's necessary to elicit the Relaxation Response. So it's important in the first phase to keep things passive and undirected. In other words, you're giving the right hemisphere of your brain complete freedom to operate and interact with your left—and to "open the door" of your mind to change.

Next, for the Principle of the Maximum Mind to become fully operative in your life, it's necessary to take the second step, to move into the second phase referred to above: You have to follow the elicitation of the Relaxation Response with a more directed form of thinking.

Here the left hemisphere of your brain will begin to come into effect again, especially if you focus or concentrate on some sort of written passage which represents the direction in which you wish your life to be heading. This more directed thought process will help you to rewire the circuits in your brain in more positive directions. Among other things, you'll find that by influencing your left hemisphere in positive ways immediately after eliciting the Relaxation Response, you'll get into the habit of making productive rather than unproductive inferences about yourself, others and your environment.

What sorts of things should you begin to focus on in this second phase of employing the Principle of the Maximum Mind?

As I've said, if you want to begin just by becoming a more positive person and if you tend to be visually oriented, you can simply focus on a happy picture. Or if you're a more verbal type, you might try reading over and over again—and thinking in a directed way upon—one or more of the following passages. I'd recommend that you pick a relatively short passage and then spend ten to fifteen minutes in pondering it and seeing how it may relate to you in a personal way. Choosing a passage that's somehow related to your personal belief system will make it even more likely that you'll begin to experience a more positive attitude.

Those of you who are biblically oriented might try one or more of these selections:

> A cheerful look brings joy to the heart and good news gives health to the bones. . . .
> Pleasant words are a honeycomb, sweet to the soul and healing to the bones. . . .

> A cheerful heart is good medicine, but a crushed spirit dries up the bones.
>
> Proverbs 15:30; 16:24; 17:22

> Finally, brethren, whatever is true, whatever is honorable, whatever is right, whatever is pure, whatever is lovely, whatever is of good repute, if there is any excellence and anything worthy of praise, let your mind dwell on these things.
>
> Philippians 4:8

> Praise God in his sanctuary;
> Praise Him in his mighty heavens;
> Praise Him for his acts of power;
> Praise Him for his surpassing greatness. . . .
> Let everything that has breath praise the Lord.
>
> Psalm 150:1–2, 6

And from the Wisdom of Ben Sira or Ecclesiasticus we find:

> Do not give yourself over to sorrow or distress yourself deliberately.
> A merry heart keeps a man alive and joy lengthens his span of days. . . .

Some may be drawn to the words of the elder statesman of positive thinking, Norman Vincent Peale. All of the following quotations are from *The Power of Positive Thinking*:

> Formulate and stamp indelibly on your mind a mental picture of yourself succeeding. Hold this picture tenaciously. Never permit it to fade. Your

mind will seek to develop this picture. Never think of yourself as failing; never doubt the reality of the mental image.

Ten times a day repeat these dynamic words, "If God be *for* us, who can be *against* us?" (Romans 8:31) (Stop reading and repeat them NOW, slowly and confidently.)

Believe that for every problem there is a solution.

Do not always ask when you pray, but instead affirm that God's blessings are being given, and spend most of your prayers giving thanks.

For the next 24 hours, deliberately speak hopefully about everything, about your job, about your health, about your future. Go out of your way to talk optimistically about everything. This will be difficult, for possibly it is your habit to talk pessimistically. From this negative habit you must restrain yourself even if it requires an act of will. . . . You must feed your mind even as you feed your body, and to make your mind healthy you must feed it nourishing, wholesome thoughts. Therefore, today start to shift your mind from negative to positive thinking. . . . Make a list of your friends to determine who is the most positive thinker among them and deliberately cultivate his society. Do not abandon your negative friends, but get closer to those with a positive point of view for a while, until you have absorbed their spirit; then you can go back among your negative friends and give them your newly acquired thought pattern without taking on their negativism.

The Reverend Robert Schuller is a more recent positive-thinking exponent. Here are some of his thoughts from his book *It's Possible* for you to consider as you move into the second phase.

> Your imagination can tranform your physical appearance! Imagine youself with twinkling eyes, a beaming face and a radiant personality. Then hold that picture in your mind, and you will become that kind of person. . . .
>
> Beauty is mind deep, not skin deep. For you are as pretty, or as ugly as you think you are. If you visualize yourself as pleasant, friendly, cheerful, laughing and with a sparkling personality, your imagination will turn you into exactly that kind of person.
>
> Begin today to exercise this positive imagination. You will discover that your smile muscles will become so strong that your facial appearance will actually be transformed!

> God has designed each of us as unique individuals and has given us the equipment and the opportunities to succeed! . . .
>
> Your life is not a happenstance, nor are you a victim of luck or fate. You are a child of God, and as you give Him your life and become an instrument of His will, nothing can stop you. You can!

> Success is not the opposite of failure. A runner may come in last, but if he beats his record time, he is a success! . . .
>
> Super-successful people know the secret. Suc-

cess is only measured by what you are, not by what you have. Everyone has within himself the potential for that kind of success!

A possibility thinker never says no to any idea that holds some possibility for good! . . .

Of all the persons living on planet Earth, there is only one person who has the power to cast the deciding vote to kill your dream. That person is you! You can also cast that life-giving, hope-filled vote that says yes to your dream!

And from *Be Happy You Are Loved*:

Your freedom to choose a positive attitude is the one treasure God will let no one take from you.

If you are not of a religious nature, look over these selections on a positive approach to life.

It was only a glad "good morning,"
As she passed along the way,
But it spread the morning's glory
Over the livelong day.

Charlotte Augusta Perry,
"Good Morning"

One single positive weighs more,
You know, than negatives a score.

Matthew Prior,
"Epistle to Fleetwood Shepherd"

I am only one,
But still I am one.

I cannot do everything,
But still I can do something;
And because I cannot do everything
I will not refuse to do the something that I can do.

Edward Everett Hale,
"A Poem for the Lend-a-Hand Society"

To look up and not down,
To look forward and not back,
To look out and not in, and
To lend a hand.

Edward Everett Hale,
"Ten Times One Is Ten,"
The Rule of the Harry Wadsworth Club

Whatever you would make habitual, practice it; and if you would not make a thing habitual, do not practice it, but habituate yourself to something else.

Epictetus,
"How the Semblances of Things
Are to Be Combated"

Everyone excels in something at which another fails.

Powerful indeed is the empire of habit.

Practice is the best of all instructors.

No man is happy who does not think himself so.

Publilius Syrus

Indeed, what is there that does not appear marvelous when it comes to our knowledge for the first time? How many things, too, are looked upon as quite impossible until they've been actually effected?

Pliny the Elder,
*Natural History*, Book VII

Little strokes fell great oaks.

Benjamin Franklin,
*Poor Richard's Almanac*

Human felicity is produced not so much by great pieces of good fortune that seldom happen, as by little advantages that occur every day.

Benjamin Franklin,
*Autobiography*

He has achieved success who has lived well, laughed often and loved much.

Bessie Anderson Stanley,
*Brown Book* magazine contest, 1904

What's the use of worrying?
It never was worthwhile,
So, pack up your troubles in your old kit-bag,
And smile, smile, smile.

George Asaf, "Pack Up
Your Troubles in Your
Old Kit-Bag"

Tous les jours, à tous points de vue, je vais de mieux en mieux. (Day by day, in every way, I'm getting better and better.)

Émile Coué,
French psychotherapist

The world would be better and brighter if our teachers would dwell on the Duty of Happiness as well as on the Happiness of Duty, for we ought to be as cheerful as we can, if only because to be happy ourselves is a most effectual contribution to the happiness of others.

Sir John Lubbock,
Lord Abebury, "The Pleasures of Life"

As a last example, you might find the following useful: after you have completed eliciting the Relaxation Response, walk to a mirror, look at yourself and smile for several seconds!

These are just a few examples of quotations, thoughts, maxims and activities which you can use to help renew your mind in a positive way after you've elicited the Relaxation Response. You can use these suggestions or select passages which you like better or which are more suited to your belief system. In any event, whatever you pick should contain an upbeat, "can-do" message.

### *Finally. . .*

I suggest that you first pray or meditate for ten to twenty minutes, using the steps that have already been described to bring forth the Relaxation Response. This is Phase One in employing the Principle of the Maximum Mind. Next, move on *immediately* to Phase Two. Select one of the above positive passages—or choose others that are more to your liking—and read the material over several times. Think about it and ponder it from as many different angles as possible. Try to decide what it means to you personally, and how you might be able to change your life and way of thinking more to conform to this truth. Devote about five to ten minutes to this focused thinking. Then repeat this process at another point several hours later in the day.

After you've followed this procedure for as short a period as a week or so, you'll begin to notice a subtle shift in your way of thinking and acting. You'll start seeing the brighter side of life, and you'll react to others in a more hopeful, uplifting and encouraging way. In short, you'll find you're turning into a more positive person.

For some of you, this may be *the* major change that you want to bring about in your life. In other words, you know you've been too negative, and you'll be quite satisfied just to learn to experience the brighter side of things. But many other people have additional life-changing objectives in mind. For those of you who want to go even farther in incorporating the Principle of the Maximum Mind into your life, let's move on now to a consideration of how your emotional and physical well-being can be transformed for the better.

# 5.

# *Maximizing Your Health*

When you become ill, there are many options for treatment open to you. You may choose to do nothing, medicate yourself with remedies that do not require a prescription, or consult a physician. You may even decide to see a "healer." Whatever course you choose, the Principle of the Maximum Mind can help you.

Make no mistake, however: My strong bias is that you see a licensed physician. Our current practice of medicine is the best the world has ever known. For the first time in the history of mankind, we can cure pneumonia, syphilis, gonorrhea and tuberculosis. Diabetic patients can now lead relatively normal lives because of the administration of insulin. Surgery can correct what would have been fatal traumatic injuries and can restore normal appearances from disfiguring conditions. Thus, if you become ill, you should first consult with a Western physician so that you can take advantage of all of the awesome wonders of modern medicine.

Still, our modern Western scientific remedies are useful with only about 25 percent of the illnesses that bring an average patient to an average doctor. The other 75 percent are either self-limited—that is, they get better by themselves—or they are related to mind-body interactions.

Western medical practice has been obstinate in its reluctance to accept mind-body interactions, like stress, as being related to the cause and course of disease. Accordingly, these mind-body diseases fall into the cracks between what medical and surgical treatments have to offer on the one hand, and what psychiatry has to offer on the other. Furthermore, even for those illnesses which do fall in the 25 percent category that medicine can treat effectively, mind-body interactions play a part.

To better understand the relative contributions of mind-body influences to disease, consider for a moment the degree to which certain physical ailments may be influenced by mental factors.

AIDS and pneumonia are caused by infectious particles such as viruses and bacteria. Our physical state of immune strength and other factors utilized to fight off the infection may be influenced by mind-body interactions and thus alter the infection. But the primary factor involved is undoubtedly the amount of infectious agent with which the body must contend.

The situation is different with tension headaches, anxiety attacks with their symptoms of nausea, vomiting, diarrhea, constipation, short-temperedness, in-

| | HYPERTENSION | |
|---|---|---|
| | MIGRAINE HEADACHES | TENSION HEADACHES |
| PNEUMONIA | ASTHMA | ANXIETY DISORDERS |
| AIDS | ULCERS | PHOBIAS |

LITTLE ——————————————————— MUCH

**Contribution of Mind-Body Interaction to Wellness**

somnia and phobias. These ailments are greatly influenced by mind-body interactions.

Other diseases such as hypertension, migraine headaches, asthma, and peptic ulcers have a more intermediate mind-body involvement.

Of course it's very difficult to be exact in determining how much influence mind-body interactions have in any given illness. To the extent that there are such influences, the Principle of the Maximum Mind is extremely beneficial. Thus, in some cases, the use of the Principle is curative in itself. In others, it can markedly improve the disorder. In yet other diseases, its use will make a patient feel better but will have little influence on the course of the disease.

Some of the disorders in which the Principle of the Maximum Mind is useful include:

- anxiety attacks;
- phobias, including debilitating fears of various types;
- asthma;
- various types of severe bodily pain;
- migraine headaches;
- high blood pressure;

- angina pectoris, or heart-related chest pains;
- immunological disorders;
- backache; and
- a variety of other stress-related ailments.

How does the Principle of the Maximum Mind help? First, you must open the door to change through the Relaxation Response and then rewire your brain through the methods that I've been describing.

For purposes of this discussion, I've separated some of the factors operative in the Principle of the Maximum Mind into three areas: pain, emotional disorders and stress. It's important for you to understand something more about each of these three factors before you attempt to make improvements in your own health.

### *The Pain Factor*

Pain is subjective—its experience literally resides in the mind. A person's state of mind, including a belief in vulnerability to pain, is thus inexorably linked to the feelings of pain. For example, if you believe for any reason that you're going to start hurting in some part of your body, the chances are greatly increased that you *will* start hurting.

This is not the whole story. Just as your mental activity can produce pain, it can also alleviate pain. And some effective means for reducing or eliminating pain in the body begin with the elicitation of the Relaxation Response.

Consider a recent study done by Dr. Andy T. Wielgosz and Dr. JoAnne Earp of the Ottawa General Hospital Department of Medicine in Canada. These researchers investigated 106 patients, 63 women and 43 men, who were preoccupied with heart and coronary illness.

As part of the study, the patients underwent coronary angiography, which involved taking X-ray pictures of their coronary arteries to establish whether or not there was any blockage or clogging from hardening of the arteries. They were experiencing chest pains characteristic of angina pectoris, and their physicians wanted to be certain about the exact state of their heart blood vessels. None of the patients showed any significant blockage in their main coronary arteries. As a matter of fact, they were classified as having a very low risk of either cardiac death or a nonfatal heart attack. Nevertheless, they continued to be afflicted with chest pains that demanded medical attention.

The researchers contacted these patients a few days after their angiography and asked them a series of questions to assess their beliefs, behaviors and expectations about the health of their heart and arteries.

When the patients—who had been told they did not suffer from coronary artery disease after the medical examination—were asked what they thought was the cause of their illness, 59 percent still responded that it was a problem with their hearts. Another 29 percent believed that they had had a heart attack in the past—although half of those patients admitted they had never been told that. Also, despite little or no evidence of coronary disease, 23 percent felt there was a high probability that they would develop a heart disease over the next five to ten years.

The researchers contacted the patients about a year later to see how they were doing, especially as far as their chest pains were concerned. Their findings? One quarter of the patients were completely pain free. The pains of another 38 percent were less. On the other hand, 30 percent of the patients had the same pains they had felt at the beginning of the study, and 7 percent reported a worsening of their symptoms. None of these patients, however, had suffered any heart attacks during this year of follow-up.

Finally, the researchers compared the current pain symptoms of the patients with the beliefs and attitudes which they had expressed one year earlier. This resulted in the discovery of a clear relationship between the patient's perception of his or her coronary vulnerability and the degree of pain. In other words, those who reported unimproved chest pains one year after the angiography were also the ones who believed that they had, or would have, a serious heart problem.

Belief, then, clearly makes a difference in the feelings of pain in our bodies. Just as belief or attitude may cause pain, our mental processes can also reduce or eliminate painful sensations. And many effective treatments involve the use of the Relaxation Response and the Principle of the Maximum Mind. Increasingly, in clinical settings, physicians are employing procedures that elicit the Relaxation Response to alleviate pain. These procedures have had to meet certain requirements to establish themselves as valid therapies. Specifically, there are three requirements or tests.

**Test #1:** Are the changes that the proposed therapy produces of significant magnitude?

If your pain can only be reduced by about 10 percent through a certain procedure, then the therapy has limited value.

**Test #2:** Can the procedure be transferred from a

laboratory or hospital setting to a normal day-to-day environment?

If a therapy requires a special research setting or much medical supervision, then it's not going to be particularly useful for the average person.

**Test #3:** Will the proposed therapy work over a relatively long period of time?

In general, any therapy that's going to be used to reduce pain must be able to work over a period of many months or even years. Short-term solutions are not desirable and better therapies therefore may be more usefully sought.

When the techniques which elicit the Relaxation Response were exposed to these three requirements, the results were rather impressive. In a series of investigations performed by Dr. John Kabat-Zinn at the University of Massachusetts, one group of patients, suffering from chronic pain, was treated by ordinary medical means over a ten-week period. They showed no significant relief. A second group in the study, comparable to the first group, was put on a meditation program designed to elicit the Relaxation Response.

In this investigation, the meditating group showed marked alleviation of pain, while the other group experienced no significant pain relief. According to a pain-rating index which the researchers devised, the pain levels in the meditating group were reduced by more than 33 percent in 72 percent of the patients. Also, 61 percent of that group had a reduction in pain of more than 50 percent.

Follow-up studies, done after fifteen months, showed that the duration of the pain-reducing benefits in the Relaxation Response group continued. In addition, the Relaxation Response skills which this group had learned were transferable to their home environment, where they practiced the therapies on their own, without any medical supervision.

Other studies have shown that similar techniques for eliciting the Relaxation Response have produced dramatic pain relief from headaches, and especially tension headaches. Migraine and other vascular headaches were also significantly alleviated. These investigations, by the way, have focused on a variety of different methods for eliciting the Relaxation Response—and there has been no clear evidence that one technique is superior to the others. In other words, if you want to meditate using Christian, Jewish or Hindu prayers or nonreligious phrases or activities, you can expect essentially the same health results, at least as far as the direct benefits of the Relaxation Response are concerned.

How, exactly, does the Relaxation Response produce this relief from pain?

That's a difficult question to answer. But a number of interesting explanations are being explored in current research. One hypothesis suggests that the elicitation of the Relaxation Response releases endorphins which suppress pain. Another hypothesis is related to alpha-wave production during elicitation of the Relaxation Response. The Relaxation Response produces an intensification of the slow alpha waves in the brain. Interestingly, pain usually suppresses the alpha-wave activity in the brain. When the Relaxation Response is elicited during an experience of pain, the Relaxation Response brings back the alpha-wave activity. Simultaneously, the pain is either reduced or eliminated.

Also, the *belief* on the part of the patient that this type of treatment is going to work contributes further to the relief of pain. To enhance relief, the patient should continue to *expect* to improve after the elicitation of the Relaxation Response. In many cases, this expectation can intensify as the person is exposed to a doctor's comforting and encouraging words or information. As one's expectation of improvement increases, further relief occurs.

In short, pain diminishes as additional ingredients of the Principle of the Maximum Mind become operative. Before long, the deeply ingrained patterns that often sustain the pain get altered and redirected—and the pain recedes further and may completely disappear.

### *The Emotional Factor*

If you have an emotional problem—or a physical problem which is rooted in a mind-body interaction—psychotherapy may provide help. Increasingly, however, psychotherapists are exploring how the methods to elicit the Relaxation Response can be combined with traditional therapy techniques.

In the Eastern religious traditions, and especially in Buddhism, great emphasis is placed upon the importance of understanding one's own psychology. This psychology, called the Abhidhamma, involves a complex analysis of the workings of the human mind in thoughts, emotions and behavior. Buddhists feel it's important to understand how their own personal psychology works before they can hope to attain higher states of consciousness. Similarly, in the Western tradition, many people turn to psychotherapy to gain a greater understanding of themselves. Then, they believe, they will be able to move on to a greater inner equilibrium, happiness and satisfaction.

In Buddhism, however—unlike Western psychotherapy—the key to understanding one's psychology has been meditation. Buddhist meditators have learned that they can open the door to changes in their minds and bodies through several meditative techniques, all of which elicit the Relaxation Response. One is known as concentration meditation. Another, more advanced form of meditation is called mindfulness meditation.

In our discussion of the basic techniques for eliciting the Relaxation Response, we've already seen how concentration meditation works. Basically, this involves focusing your attention on a single repetitive word, sound, prayer, phrase, visual object or breathing process. Then when the mind wanders to everyday thoughts, the meditator passively disregards the intrusion and refocuses his attention on the key word, sound or other activity. In this way, the meditator leaves logical thought behind and moves deeper and deeper into a distinctive state, which we have designated as the Relaxation Response.

With mindfulness meditation, in contrast, the meditator focuses more on the emotional and mental processes going on inside him—much as a person would do under the direction of a psychotherapist. But there are some definite differences from psychotherapy. In mindfulness meditation, you first establish awareness of your breathing: that is, you elicit the Relaxation Response. Once this state has been established, you begin to observe in a detached fashion the procession of thoughts and mental images that go on inside of you.

Unlike concentration meditation, then, mindfulness meditation involves allowing your attention to leave the repetitive word, phrase or activity and to shift freely from one perception to the next. You don't regard any thoughts or sensations as intrusions. Rather, when they drift into your mind you observe them in a detached way, instead of gently disregarding them as you would in concentration meditation.

Some may assume that mindfulness meditation is a lot like regular thinking or daydreaming. That's not so. Unlike these practices, mindfulness meditation is designed to keep you from becoming totally involved with the mental content of your thoughts. Rather, you're supposed to maintain the perspective of an observer. If you *do* become lost in your thoughts, you must focus once more on your breathing in an effort to regain the detached observation point from which you were following your thoughts, images or emotions.

Those experienced in such forms of meditation eventually go beyond specific thoughts and images and begin to recognize patterns and habits that influence their thoughts and actions. For example, if such a meditator experiences anger, he learns to deal with it in a detached way. First, he'll notice the fact that he's angry. Then, he won't continue to feel, "I am angry." Instead, he'll deal with it more as an observer—such as by saying, "There is anger inside me." By thus approaching his emotions at a distance, the meditator will place himself in a better position to understand those emotions and to deal with them constructively.

Among other things, those advanced in mindfulness meditation often experience an intensified perceptual awareness of objects, thoughts and emotions. This greater vividness of inner experience can bring a heightened awareness and new meaning to old habits and thoughts. Also, the brain's plasticity, or ability to change, which we've already discussed in some detail, becomes more pronounced. As a result, the individual is able to handle data, both about the outside world and about himself, more effectively and creatively.

Throughout this entire process of meditation, there is a sense of "letting go" which meditators and others experienced in spiritual matters frequently describe. Shackles that the left hemisphere of the brain imposes on our consciousness and actions fall away in this heightened emotional state. A kind of defenselessness or vulnerability accompanies the process, with a soothing sense of well-being near at hand. Emotions such as fear, love, anger and joy, which may have been blocked or suppressed, come to the surface. And they usually emerge in a way that the individual can deal with much more easily.

This entire process of mindfulness meditation can provide what's been called a "primer for psychotherapy." The mental doors are open to greater insights and creativity—and the way is paved to escape from past obsessions, compulsions or bad habits. The connection of this process of meditation with the techniques and goals of psychotherapy is obvious.

For these and other reasons, I recommend that meditation and psychotherapy be combined in the treatment of many patients with emotional and stress-related physical ills. You, as a potential patient, should keep certain cautionary principles in mind.

First of all, when you combine psychotherapy and

meditation, you're greatly enhancing the power of your brain and your life to be changed. In other words, you'll be opening yourself to major transformation through increasing the plasticity of your mind. At the same time, if you're involved in psychotherapy, you'll find that you're already receiving the help of a kind of maximum mind guide in the form of your psychotherapist or psychologist. He or she is essential and will be providing some subtle and not-so-subtle influences to hasten and increase the changes that are going on inside you.

Clearly it's extremely important for you to know who your psychotherapist or psychologist is and what value systems he or she is trying to promote. You can be sure of one thing: Every psychotherapist has a point of view as far as basic beliefs and values are concerned.

I'm aware of several cases where psychotherapists were as disposed toward their patient's divorce as toward saving the marriage. The main value which these therapists upheld was the right of the individual to control his own destiny and personal potential. But suppose the patient has a value system which emphasizes keeping a marriage together, even if it means making certain sacrifices of one's individual potential? The values of the psychotherapist and patient should not come into conflict. Through the increased susceptibility of the patient to being changed, the values of the therapist might prevail—and the patient's fundamental value system would be undermined.

I'm not offering any suggestions about what any specific psychotherapist should advise a patient in a particular situation. I am saying that it's wise to understand what your psychotherapist's values are before you place yourself under his or her care. This caution is especially important if you plan to open yourself up to change through a maximum mind technique.

It's as important to take a great deal of care in this decision as it is in the choice of a meditative word or phrase to use in eliciting the Relaxation Response. Both your meditative phrase *and* the philosophy of your maximum mind guide should have roots that run deep into your own basic belief system.

### *The Stress Factor*

More and more, scientific evidence tends to show that the pressures and stresses of life can have a devastating impact on one's emotional and physical health. Obviously, there is a pronounced mind-body interaction in the terrible influences that stress can have in our lives. I have extensively documented these effects in my previous books.

In one Swedish study published in 1986, 159 patients who suffered stomach pain for at least two months a year were tested to see what might relieve their discomfort. The patients were divided into three groups: The first received a very popular prescription drug; the second, a common over-the-counter antacid solution; and the third, a placebo. After a three-week period, *all* the patients experienced about the same degree of relief—or approximately a 25 percent decrease in the severity or frequency of their stomach pains.

The researchers concluded in this study that the patient's belief in the treatment, rather than any special curative value of the medicines, was the key to the relief of stress. One of them said, "We can't find anything wrong with about half the people coming to us complaining of stomach pain. . . . We're beginning to think stress is the problem, that it's a mind-gut interaction, in which case all the acid-inhibiting drugs in the world won't work."

Another way that stress may undercut our health is by attacking our immune systems. In fact, a new discipline of science, psychoneuroimmunology, has evolved to bring together the disciplines of psychology, neurology and immunology. According to one summary report from the American Association for the Advancement of Science, immune functions may be impaired in people who are under various degrees of stress. These include divorced and separated women and medical students facing exams. But these immunological problems can be reversed by using the Relaxation Response and positive-thinking techniques. All this provides further evidence of connections between stress, and the central nervous system and the immune system.

Inner and outer pressures may cause stress which can have both physical and emotional manifestations in our bodies. How, in more precise terms, does stress interact with the brain and mind?

One explanation suggests that certain parts of the brain are the sites of anxiety-provoked reactions. These areas may become extremely sensitive and more susceptible to arousal by repeated exposure to internal and external pressures.

This neurologic hypersensitivity, as it's called, may involve a process known as "kindling" in the brain tissues. Kindling refers to the phenomenon of repeated stimulation of certain parts of the brain that results in a sensitizing of those parts. They respond to less stimulation and more powerfully to normal stimulation. Thus repeated exposure to stresses and pressures activate the arousal mechanisms of the brain and make arousal more likely in ways that are physically and emotionally debilitating. In other words, some individuals, whose brains have been kindled or sensitized, may be inclined to experience serious anxiety or panic attacks more readily than others who are less sensitized.

On the biological level, as this excessive stimulation occurs, the brain cells actually tend to make use of more dendrites in response to the stimulation. With such changes in the brain, the situation can get worse and worse. New neural pathways or wirings develop so that the individual gets into the habit of responding excessively to the various stresses.

In animals, it usually takes a number of repeated stimulations or stresses of this type, occurring within twenty-four hours of each other, to induce the kindling response and the subsequent changes in the physical structure of the brain. After sufficient changes have occurred in this plastic mental mechanism, the increased sensitivity to the stress may last for hours, days or even months.

This is not the end of the matter. Just as the brain can change in negative ways as a result of stress, it can also return to a more positive set of pathways. Researchers have found that there's some tendency for any hypersensitivity in the brain to *diminish* over a period of days or months—provided there is no more stimulation or stress of the type that caused the problem in the first place.

In other words, if you're experiencing bad physical

or emotional reactions to stress or pressures in your life, you should probably do everything possible to *avoid* the source of those pressures for a period of time.

Sometimes, it's just not possible to escape or run away. Even if we do avoid various pressures and stress-inducing situations, we may be dissatisfied with the speed of our emotional and physical recovery. To speed the process along, Dr. George Everly of the University of Maryland advises that it's helpful to rely on certain "relaxation technologies" as therapy.

As he says, "Only recently, within the last decade, have relaxation-oriented therapies been considered as interventions that may have a therapeutic 'main effect.' . . . The possibility that we will discover, someday, that anxiety disorders and perhaps other arousal-like disorders may be 'biological' in nature *in no way* negates, nor minimizes, the applicability of 'behavioral' therapeutic interventions."

In other words, your brain may develop negative pathways and wirings as a result of the stresses of life. In such a case, a physical change takes place inside you, as you feel anxieties, worries and obsessions mounting and being expressed as physical ailments in your body. A treatment for this type of disorder is to elicit the Relaxation Response and then make use of the Principle of the Maximum Mind.

• • •

Let's turn now to some specific illustrations of how the Principle of the Maximum Mind, grounded solidly in the Relaxation Response, can relieve various physical and emotional problems. As we proceed through the remainder of the book, I'll include a number of other case studies that involve the health-enhancing effects of the Principle of the Maximum Mind. At this point, however, I just want to highlight a few major health problems where the Principle has proved effective.

**Health Problem #1: Angina pectoris (heart-related chest pains).** Over the centuries, patients with angina pectoris pain have found relief through a variety of different treatments, many of which seem to have had no particular connection with the others, except that patients, and often physicians, have believed deeply in the ability of a particular treatment to work, and there has been a sound doctor-patient relationship.

In our own day, we're finding that belief is just as powerful as it ever was. When we can combine that belief with a stress-relieving technique, we often find we have an answer to reducing or eliminating angina pains. An excellent, succinct example of the way this works can be found in the experience of one of my patients, who described her personal experience this way.

"Ten years ago, I was diagnosed as having angina. The pains have come and gone [since then]. But recently, they gradually appeared with greater frequency and intensity.

"Over a year ago, I had such severe chest pains that I was hospitalized for four days. Since then, I've continued to have chest pains off and on—until about twelve months ago. At that time, I began practicing meditation twice a day, as my doctor taught me. The meditation phrase 'Christ have mercy' brings a special sense of peace and comfort to me. My faith has been the source of my strength throughout my life."

Despite her very serious past history of angina,

today she no longer suffers chest pain. She still utilizes medication, but less than she had used previously. In this case, the woman opened the door for her mind to be changed and arranged her life to encourage the pain-inducing pathways to be rerouted.

How, exactly, did this occur? First of all, quite wisely, she decided to root her meditative technique in her own belief system—the Christian faith. She kept in close touch with me during the first phases of practicing the meditative technique as well, and I became her maximum mind guide, helping provide reinforcement for the beneficial changes which were already beginning to take place in her mind. Also, she did not abandon the standard medical treatments.

As with many such health problems, it wasn't really necessary for this woman to get too specific in thinking about or focusing upon the exact change that she wanted to take place in her mind and body. She didn't have to "visualize" the precise changes she wanted in her body. All she had to do was encourage the process of change by relying on her basic beliefs, and then follow closely her physician's advice. The reduction in her chest pains followed naturally from this process.

**Health Problem #2: High blood pressure.** We've had considerable clinical success in lowering high blood pressure using the Principle. One of my patients came to me with elevated blood pressure and a variety of other physical and emotional problems. Like many other people, he had a long history of negative wiring in his brain to overcome.

This man had led a rather active, athletic life when he was younger. As he got older and closer to forty, he began to develop health problems.

He experienced a sudden pain in his chest one day and immediately checked with his doctor. He was told there was nothing wrong with him. The pain recurred, and he went back to the doctor again, only to be told once more that there was nothing wrong with him. Finally, his physician referred him to a psychiatrist.

"The psychiatrist suggested I go away and be alone, isolated from people for several weeks," the man recalled.

As we've already seen, avoiding stimulations and pressures which may produce stress or anxiety may help the sensitized parts of our brains to return to normal—and emotional and physical ills to disappear. This isolation or withdrawal approach didn't work in this particular person's case. Instead, he got worse.

"I began to have fears that there were all kinds of things wrong with me," he said. "These fears kept growing and growing. Eventually I could not go on elevators, over bridges, through tunnels. I couldn't even leave my house unless someone came with me. It was impossible for me to go away on vacations because of all these fears—which included flying."

This man was beset by a variety of phobias which completely debilitated him. To top it all off, he developed higher blood pressure readings. Now, quite worried about the downhill direction in which his health seemed to be heading, he consulted a number of other doctors, trying to find an effective treatment. Each of them prescribed various types of medication, but that was bothersome. For one thing, he had side effects from the medication and the very fact that he needed medication disturbed him even more. It reinforced his fears about the possible consequences of suffering from high blood pressure. These fears in turn made his blood pressure still higher. He was caught in a vicious cycle.

Finally he came to our offices. We continued his medication and put him on a meditation program based on his religious background. In addition, we assigned him to a maximum mind guide, a physician who could monitor his progress.

"Within one month, I started to feel wonderful," the man reported.

He wasn't "cured" of all his ailments overnight. It had taken him twenty years to get to the state he was in when he entered our offices; so we couldn't expect to send him out a new man after one or two sessions. In fact, he's been under treatment in our offices for about three years. During that time his progress has been remarkable.

"I have learned to look at my fears even while meditating, and with the wonderful help of [my doctor], I have overcome *99 percent* of my fears."

He goes on to point out that he's flown to California several times in the past three years; he has no trouble with elevators, bridges or tunnels anymore; and he can now travel alone almost anywhere without any problem.

"At one time I could not drive to see my doctor unless someone accompanied me," he says. "Now, what a wonderful feeling I experience as I'm driving anywhere, all by myself, with a big smile on my face. It's great to be alive!"

The man's blood pressure has now returned to normal, and he needs little medication.

Obviously, this is a major success story, but it's not an isolated example. Even a person with so many emotional and physical problems can expect to see significant and even dramatic progress. It just requires a decision to follow the simple disciplines required with employing the Principle of the Maximum Mind.

This man opened his mind and habits to change by eliciting the Relaxation Response. Then, he pursued meditative techniques that were related to his belief system, under the regular supervision of a director—a physician in our offices. The presence of a medical expert, who symbolized the hope and possibility of the recovery of his physical and emotional health, was a constant positive influence in his life as his health improved.

**Health Problem #3: Phobias.** As the previous example shows, the Principle of the Maximum Mind can be quite effective in dealing with phobias combined with other ailments. As a variation on that theme, let's turn now to a "purer" phobia illustration—one which demonstrates a classic application of the Principle of the Maximum Mind.

Mike, a successful New York businessman who had risen to the level of senior vice president in a large corporation, suddenly found himself confronted with a rather embarrassing situation. While on a recent business trip to Europe, he went downstairs to visit a small restaurant in Paris and found himself being seated in an ovenlike room in which all the walls seemed to be closing in on him. There were no windows, and he was facing away from the only entrance. The crowds in the room grew larger and larger and the cigarette smoke hung heavily in the air.

Suddenly Mike, who had always felt mildly uncomfortable in closed places, underwent a severe attack of claustrophobia. His breath began to come in short gasps; his stomach felt as though it were coming up into his throat; and he knew that if he didn't get out of that room as soon as possible he would "flip out." Mumbling some excuse about having forgotten another appointment, he rushed away from his luncheon companions and soon was leaning against a post on the sidewalk, gasping for air.

After this experience, Mike found that the claustrophobia seemed to get worse. He couldn't tolerate crowded elevators, and he even had trouble sitting in the backseats of cars which lacked backseat doors. Obviously, this problem that he was developing could get embarrassing if he had to go with business companions to closed-in restaurants, ride in elevators, take trips in coupe-type cars or get into any other situation in which he felt enclosed.

Mike managed to make it through this particular business trip without any further crises relating to his claustrophobia. When he got back home, he immediately described his problem to a close friend in his church. Fortunately, the friend was familiar with some of the basic techniques involved in employing the Principle of the Maximum Mind. Specifically, he told Mike to take these steps:

- Pray to ask God to help you overcome this problem.
- Then meditate on a passage of Scripture—preferably one that is meaningful to you, but not necessarily one connected with the claustrophobia.
- After fifteen or twenty minutes of this meditation, ask God to draw your eye to another passage of Scripture which may somehow be related to good health or

even to this problem of claustrophobia. When you find the passage, focus on it; think about it deeply; and try to see practical ways that it may apply to the problem you're facing.

- When you find yourself in another closed-in situation, imagine that Jesus Himself is right there with you, comforting you and supporting you.

Mike was a little skeptical because he had never tried praying and meditating in quite this way before. But he trusted his friend—who now had become a spiritual director for him with this problem. So he decided to give it a try.

He chose the meditative phrase "God is love," from the first epistle of John. Then, as he began to look through some of his favorite Biblical passages to use after the twenty-minute period of meditation, he settled upon a section of Psalm 139: "Where can I go from thy spirit? Or where can I flee from thy presence? . . . If I take the wings of the dawn, if I dwell in the remotest part of the sea, even there thy hand will lead me, and thy right hand will lay hold of me" (Psalm 139:7, 9–10).

Mike followed this meditative procedure for several days, and it was all very comforting. But he had yet to face the test to see how it would apply in practice. He got his chance later.

He had been invited to ride in the backseat of a very tight little sportscar to a restaurant on the top of one of Manhattan's tallest buildings. He knew that when he would be going up in the elevator, the crowds would still be heavy from the rush hour. He had already experienced several days of meditation and mind-changing exercises. Also, he remembered his friend's advice to imagine that Jesus was right there with him, as he rode in the backseat of that car and went up on the elevator. He even added a little twist of his own: He practiced his regular breathing exercises, with the "God is love" focus phrase, while he was in those stressful situations.

Mike's recovery turned out to be rather rapid. He did experience a few twinges of anxiety as he entered the car and then moved into the elevator. But he had prepared well, and he really believed the technique was going to work. As a result, he was relatively at ease during the entire evening.

Mike continued to practice these same techniques for a number of weeks, and he was equally successful in dealing with several other claustrophobic situations during that period. Currently, he has returned to the same level of nonphobic emotional health that he enjoyed before that disconcerting experience in Paris.

As I said at the beginning of this example, Mike's case presents an almost classic illustration of how the Principle of the Maximum Mind can work to combat phobias. This claustrophobia was a problem of very short duration, and undoubtedly that was one of the major reasons he was able to rid himself of it so quickly. Still, he needed the motivation and discipline to use these various techniques conscientiously—and he quickly reaped the benefits. If you are suffering from phobias or any other problems which are deeply rooted and go back many years, you may have to stick with the treatment process for a longer period of time. But I'm convinced that many can eventually expect the same kind of success that Mike enjoyed.

**Health Problem #4: Insomnia.** Many people in our

society have trouble falling asleep at night, especially as they get older. Often, the problem is that we develop "worry loops" in our minds: We begin to think about some problem or issue just before bedtime, and then we "play that mental tape" over and over again in our heads after we lie down to try to sleep. The fatigue at the end of the day, combined with the increased anxiety over the problem on our minds, sometimes makes it impossible to settle down and fall asleep.

A number of people have found that merely eliciting the Relaxation Response in a supine position in bed is enough to induce sleep in just a few minutes. Others, though, are sometimes so agitated at bedtime that they simply can't settle down enough to get involved in such focused thinking. One solution to this more serious problem is to get into the habit of meditating or praying during the day; this practice tends to lay the groundwork for greater ease of focusing thought and easier sleep at night. In this way, we encourage change in the mental pathways that are creating anxiety and keeping us awake. Then, restful sleep can ensue.

Arlene, a professional woman in her forties, had been having trouble with getting to sleep since she was a teenager. It would usually take her at least thirty minutes, and sometimes three to four hours, to fall asleep. Further, she would wake up two or three times during the night, go to the bathroom, and then return to bed and try to fall asleep again.

Then, when she passed thirty years of age, a new pattern developed. "I would wake up early in the morning, usually between two and four A.M., and then not be able to get back to sleep for one to two hours," she said. "Occasionally, I'd lie awake until it was time to get up at about seven."

Arlene's problem was exacerbated by the fact that she had two children during this period and found she had to wake up at night many times during their infancy to take care of them. After her younger child was old enough to sleep through the night, Arlene couldn't break the habit of getting up even more often during the early morning hours.

Here we have an example of the kindling process that goes on inside our brains at one time or another. Arlene apparently became exceptionally sensitive to insomnia during this period because her brain was stimulated consistently, both by her own longstanding tendencies to stay awake at night, and also by the outside pressures of being the mother of very young children. We hypothesize that her brain cells grew new tentacles, which made this sensitivity—and insomnia—a deeply rooted part of her life.

Fortunately, Arlene chose to try a Relaxation Response technique to help her overcome this problem. She sought out a physician who understood how to elicit the Relaxation Response through a meditative technique—one which was rooted in her own humanistic philosophy of life. In her case, she chose a few lyrical words from one of her favorite poems as her special meditative phrase. Then, after she had elicited the Relaxation Response, she would often read a larger portion of one of these favorite poems—especially one which tended to have some soothing, peaceful message.

Her physician encouraged her to elicit the Relaxation Response in this way at least once a day, with rather dramatic results. In only one week, she found that even if she woke up at two or four in the morning, she would go right back to sleep. She even discovered that she didn't need to get up to go to the bathroom during the night, as she'd had to do ever since she was a teenager.

"My biggest problem now is maintaining a daily regimen of the Relaxation Response," she says. "It seems to make a difference in my sleep habits, but I get casual about it—that is, it stops being a top priority for me. Then I find I'm sleeping badly again, and I resolve once more to do it regularly, and so on and so on."

This woman may be an excellent example of how the kindling concept works. Since her youth, she had been developing habits or patterns which interfered with her sleep. In neurological terms, she could well have established dendrites or tentacles in certain sections of her brain which made her extra sensitive to the stresses and strains that kept her awake.

Then, she began to break through the negative patterns by eliciting the Relaxation Response under the guidance of a maximum mind guide, her physician. And she further influenced her more positive mental development through soothing poetic readings.

Before long, the "insomnia-sensitized" dendrites in her brain had receded, and sleep came more easily. At the same time, however, she remained susceptible to slipping back into old patterns—especially when she "got casual," as she put it, about eliciting the Relaxation Response and employing the Principle of the Maximum Mind.

**Health Problem #5: Anxiety.** It's been said that

we live in an age of anxiety, and I heartily agree that the pressures that constantly bombard us are a distinctive characteristic of our era. Most important of all, we really don't know how to handle these anxieties; far too often we let them get the best of us.

There's a way out. In one rather extreme case, a seventy-year-old woman told me, "I had a long history of anxiety that at times was overwhelming and incapacitating."

She tried many different solutions:

"Valium just dulled my feelings a little."

"I had professional therapy."

"I attended self-help groups—and these gave me some relief. But it wasn't enough to make my days bearable."

"I was seeing at least one physician every week."

Finally, as a last resort, she decided to undergo treatment by a doctor who taught a technique which elicited the Relaxation Response. As her focus word, she chose the Hebrew word for peace, "Shalom." Unfortunately, her long background of anxiety ran so deep that she didn't experience rapid improvement.

"It's the understatement of the year to say that it was difficult for me to sit patiently and try to relax," she said. "I will admit it took me a long time, and on many occasions my thoughts were, What's the use? I can't do it! It isn't helping!"

To make matters worse, this woman suffered from tinnitus—noise kept ringing in one of her ears. This tended to distract her and kept her from being effective with her meditation.

She kept at it for more than a year. "With determination and persistence—and meditating three times a day—I gradually noticed that my heartbeat and pulse began to slow down," she said. "Also, I was feeling less and less anxious. Wonder of wonders!"

From her point of view the change was so spectacular that she said, "I still can't believe that I went through all that suffering and now I'm able to control my anxiety and impatience."

She no longer takes Valium or any other medication.

In this particular case, a maximum mind guide in the form of a physician was an extremely important factor in this woman's recovery. She trusted the doctor who taught her the Relaxation Response technique which conformed to her belief system. She also listened closely to his explanations of the probable causes of her anxiety. Soon, she began to understand how that anxiety was being overcome by the changes that were taking place inside her brain. The doctor, acting after the Relaxation Response had opened the door of her mind to change, educated her as to the practical benefits that she could expect in her life. The final result was significant change.

**Health Problem #6: Healing of painful memories.** Here we begin to get into an area which is practically impossible to quantify scientifically. We can only listen to the reports of relief which come from those whose painful memories really have been healed. In many ways, this healing of memories is what psychotherapy strives for. A psychiatrist or psychologist will lead a person back into his or her earlier life in search of the causes of disturbances and problems which have cropped up later. With greater understanding of his or her past, the patient can move ahead toward emotional health.

The guide in memory healing doesn't always have to be a certified psychotherapist or psychiatrist. In fact, with less serious problems, other nonprofessional guides can often do just as well as qualified therapists. Take the case of a young man, Arthur, who was frequently mildly depressed and seemed to live with a constant cloud hanging over his life, though he couldn't identify the cause of his emotional pall.

Arthur was a firm Christian and a believer in the power of prayer. But prayer somehow didn't seem to solve his problems, no matter how often he offered up his supplications to God. So he went to a friend, who was also a Christian believer, and was advised to try a meditative technique using a Bible verse, "The Lord is my shepherd," as his focus phrase.

Arthur did elicit the Relaxation Response through this technique over a period of several weeks—and consequently, he managed to "prime" his mind for major change. When the two friends met, the older Christian, who had now become Arthur's spiritual director, began the session with a time of joint meditation and prayer.

Gently but firmly the director began to encourage the younger man to probe back into his earlier life to try to determine if the source of depression and lethargy might lie there. Over a period of about an hour, long-suppressed memories began to open up. Arthur had experienced a form of "childhood amnesia," in that he had completely forgotten some traumatic incidents that had happened when he was a preschooler. Specifically, he had been sexually abused on a number of occasions by an older boy. It was at that point that the spark went out of his life and a tendency to be depressed and lethargic set it.

Now the pathway to healing was open. With the new knowledge of what had happened to him in those early years, he was able to confront his situation more directly and employ other spiritual tools to which his faith gave him access. For one thing, at the urging of his spiritual director, he explicitly forgave the boy who had abused him as a youngster. Also, he prayed that God would heal those wounds which had been opened again in such a way that he could begin to lead a normal life.

In Arthur's case, remembering the child abuse incidents was just the beginning of a process which would take months to reach even the semblance of completion. Still, he began to show regular, gradual improvement in his attitudes and in his emotional life.

Examples of this type have been and continue to be repeated over and over again in pastoral counseling, in psychotherapy sessions and in less formal meetings between lay people. When the procedures are conducted sensitively and persistently, positive results can be obtained, regardless of who is taking on the role of maximum mind guide.

In such cases, the mind is opened for change by the elicitation of the Relaxation Response through prayer and meditation. Sometimes, as in Arthur's case, it's helpful to prepare the mind with a series of meditation sessions for several days or even weeks before any attempt is made to delve more deeply into the closed-off memories. Once that preliminary process has been completed—and once the mental doors have swung open—the possibilities for change through the Principle of the Maximum Mind are astounding.

### *How to Renew Your Own Health*

Now let's turn to you—to your emotional and physical health. Do you have a problem that's bothering you? Do you perhaps suffer from some form of insomnia, a particular phobia or some degree of anxiety? Or could it be that you experience intermittent headaches or other physical discomforts? If so, and *to the extent that your health problems are influenced by mind-body interactions, the Principle of the Maximum Mind may be very advantageous for you.*

I want to make it clear, once again, that the Relaxation Response treatments that I'm suggesting here are not necessarily a substitute for medicine. In fact, if you're under medical treatment, it's very important for you to continue consulting with your physician as you use the Principle of the Maximum Mind. Obviously, under these conditions, your physician becomes a maximum mind guide. You may need medical prescriptions or even surgery in addition to a Relaxation Response or mind-changing technique. So let your physician determine whether or not to change the medicine that you're taking and *don't* attempt to make this decision yourself.

You can then apply the Principle of the Maximum Mind and see whether your physical and emotional ills are improving as a result. If you find you're doing quite well, the chances are your physician will respond accordingly and reduce or eliminate your medication. Even if you find you can't eliminate your medication completely, it's almost certain that you'll be helped to some extent by incorporating the Principle of the Maximum Mind into your life.

Let's try applying the Principle of the Maximum Mind to the physical and emotional ailments that may be giving you trouble. As before, you should begin by eliciting the Relaxation Response.

### *Phase One*

**Step 1:** Pick a focus word or short phrase that's firmly rooted in your personal belief system.

**Step 2:** Sit quietly in a comfortable position.

**Step 3:** Close your eyes.

**Step 4:** Relax your muscles.

**Step 5:** Breathe slowly and naturally and, as you do, repeat your focus word or phrase as you exhale.

**Step 6:** Assume a passive attitude. Don't worry about how well you're doing. When other thoughts come to mind, simply say to yourself, "Oh, well," and gently return to the repetition.

**Step 7:** Continue for ten to twenty minutes.

**Step 8:** Practice the technique once or twice daily.

### *Phase Two*

Now that your mind is open to beneficial change, it's important to begin to expose yourself for ten to twenty minutes to health-oriented thoughts and information. Here are a few ideas that you might concentrate on for this phase of the Principle of the Maximum Mind. Obviously, you should choose a thought which conforms to what you believe in, or with which you are most comfortable.

It is in vain that you rise up early and
  go late to rest,
eating the bread of anxious toil;
for he gives to his beloved sleep.

Psalm 127:2

The Lord is my light and my salvation; whom shall I fear? The Lord is the stronghold [refuge] of my life; of whom shall I be afraid?

Psalm 27:1

But for those who fear My name, the sun of righteousness will rise with healing in its wings; and you will go forth and skip about like calves from the stall.

Malachi 4:2 (NASB)

Be anxious for nothing, but in everything by prayer and supplication with thanksgiving let your requests be made known to God. And the peace of God, which surpasses all comprehension, shall guard your hearts and your minds in Christ Jesus.

Finally, brethren, whatever is true, whatever is honorable, whatever is right, whatever is pure, whatever is lovely, whatever is of good repute, if there is any excellence and if anything worthy of praise, let your mind dwell on these things.

Philippians 4:6–7 and 8

Everything arises and passes away. When you see this, you are above sorrow. This is the shining way.

The Buddha

Give me health and a day, and I will make the pomp of emperors ridiculous.

Ralph Waldo Emerson,
*Nature*

My long sickness
Of health and living now begins to mend. . . .

William Shakespeare,
*Timon of Athens*

A thing of beauty is a joy forever:
Its loveliness increases; it will never
Pass into nothingness; but still will keep
A bower quiet for us, and a sleep
Full of sweet dreams, and health, and quiet breathing.

John Keats,
*Endymion*

. . . ask that Something to come into you. Just say "Whoever you are or whatever you are, come into me now and help nature in my body to mend this bone, and do it quick. Thanks, I believe you're doing it." Then, make a picture in your mind of the leg well. Shut your eyes and see it that way. See the bone all built in and the flesh strong and perfect around it. And play like you see a kind of light shining and burning and flowing all up and down the leg.

God made, first of all, *light*. Then the Spirit of God moved upon the face of the deep, so the historian tells us, doing his best to put into the words at his disposal truths that even our modern term "inter-stellar space" does not adequately express.

We are therefore made, not of solid and impenetrable matter, but of energy. The very chemicals contained in the body—the "dust of the earth"—live by the breath of God, by the primal energy, the original force that we call God. This being so, it is not strange at all that when we establish a closer connection with God in prayer, we should receive more abundant life—an increased flow of energy. The creative force that sustains us is increased within our bodies.

Agnes M. Sanford,
*The Healing Light*

. . . conquest of panic is an essential part of any recovery program from a serious disease. There is the tendency, especially if illness is prolonged, to expect the worst. Confidence, deep purpose, joyousness, laughter, and the will to live are good conditioning agents and their value should never be underestimated. At the very least, they increase the value of the medical treatment we receive.

Current scientific research in the physiological benefits of laughter may not be abundant but is significant nonetheless. William Fry, of Stanford University, has written a highly illuminating paper, "The Respiratory Components of Mirthful Laughter." I assume he is referring to what is commonly known as belly laughter. Like Immanuel Kant, Fry finds that the entire process of respiration is benevolently engaged by laughter. . . .

Some people, in the grip of uncontrollable laughter, say their ribs are hurting. The expression is probably accurate, but it is a delightful "hurt" that leaves the individual relaxed almost to the point of an open sprawl. It is a kind of "pain," too, that most people would do well to experience every day of their lives. It is as specific and tangible as any other form of physical exercise. Though its biochemical manifestations have yet to be as explicitly charted and understood as the effects of fear or frustration or rage, they are real enough.

Norman Cousins,
*Anatomy of an Illness*

Though I have patches on me pantaloons, I've ne'er a wan on me intestines.

Finley Peter Dunne,
*A Thanksgiving*

These are a few ideas and concepts which may help you begin to alter your thought patterns and habits—and embark on a new path to improved health. Of course you're quite free to substitute readings, passages or images of your own. The key is just to expose yourself to beneficial, health-promoting influences immediately after you've "opened up" your mind through the Relaxation Response.

Now let's move on to another area of life—physical fitness—where many of us could use beneficial transformation.

# 6.

## *Winning the Fight for Fitness*

A well-conditioned, high-performance body has become a symbol of personal achievement in our society. A muscled, sculpted physique—and also the ability to run, swim or cycle for hours without breathing hard—can convince us we are somehow in control of our lives.

A significant level of fitness will often provoke such comments like the following:

"He thinks enough of himself to stay in shape."

"Wow, how I'd like to have a body like hers!"

"He walks like a person with plenty of confidence."

To achieve a better physical appearance, Americans are exercising and dieting in record numbers. The Gallup Poll asked the American people in 1961 whether they engaged in physical fitness on a regular basis. Nearly a quarter at that time said they did. By 1984, the figure had increased dramatically: Nearly six out of ten adults responded that they exercised regularly. As for dealing with weight problems, about a third of all American women between the ages of nineteen and thirty-nine have told Gallup they diet at least once a month.

Even as people wage a fight for personal fitness, they remain dissatisfied. Significant numbers of both men and women continue to be unhappy about their height, weight, muscle tone and body proportions, according to a survey published in the April 1986 issue of *Psychology Today*. Half of all men and nearly six out of ten women said they were dissatisfied with their "midtorso" region. In this study, more than a third of both the men and women who responded said they were dissatisfied with their "looks as they are."

Another common complaint is that many people can't seem to get started on a regular series of workouts or a weight-reduction regimen. They just don't seem to have the self-discipline, the motivation, the interest or the time.

In other cases, people who do manage to get started sometimes "go stale." They get tired of the type of athletic activity they've chosen and it becomes drudgery to keep up with it. Still others, particularly those who have developed a certain skill in competitive sports, get frustrated because they seem to have reached a ceiling on their personal performance. They simply can't achieve the next step on the squash or tennis ladder at their club, or they can't seem to beat a weekend sports partner who has an edge on them.

Fortunately, the Principle of the Maximum Mind has an answer to these types of problems. The Principle can enable you to:

- Establish new fitness disciplines, even though you may have concluded that certain changes in your physical habits are impossible;
- Enhance your enjoyment of your chosen athletic or fitness activity; and
- Improve your performance in competitive sports, whether you're an amateur or a professional.

As with any other change in your thought patterns, a transformation of your fitness discipline depends first on your basic belief system. The achievements and frustrations of athletic endeavor can be directly influenced by the elicitation of the Relaxation Response in the context of your most deeply held beliefs.

One example of the profound effect that belief can have upon athletic experience can be seen in a case involving the Masters Two-Step Test. In this test, the patient steps up onto an elevated step or bench with one foot and then brings his other foot up next to the first one. Then he steps down with the first foot and then the other. The patient repeats the procedure in a constant series of steps, up and down, up and down. This exercise tends to raise a person's heart rate, much like a stress test conducted on modern treadmills. In fact, it was a forerunner of the treadmill. In the past, many physicians relied on the Masters Two-Step to increase heart rate under exercise conditions.

Dr. Bernard Lown, who recently received a Nobel Peace Prize for his work with Physicians for Social Responsibility, conducted a study with a man who was known to develop angina pectoris chest pains when he engaged in the Masters Two-Step. Dr. Lown found that his patient developed the angina pains on the forty-fourth count or cycle of the test. Typically, the doctor would begin out loud at "forty" and continue "forty-one, forty-two, forty-three, forty-four." Precisely at the forty-fourth count, the chest pains would occur.

After observing the patient's reactions, Dr. Lown decided to conduct an experiment. He started counting forty out loud when the real count was actually twenty-eight. In other words, he said, "forty, forty-one, forty-two, forty-three, forty-four" when in fact the actual count was "twenty-eight, twenty-nine, thirty, thirty-one, thirty-two." The true count made no difference. When he said "forty-four," his patient developed the angina pains in virtually every instance.

To test this phenomenon further, he occasionally switched back on succeeding tests to the true count, so that forty would actually be forty. In those situations, the angina pains did not develop until the physician reached the true number forty-four.

Finally, on one occasion when Dr. Lown delivered the false count, the patient said, "Doctor, either you don't know how to count, or else you're finagling—it's only twenty-eight." Thereafter, the patient experienced no anginal pain at the lower count.

This simple illustration shows that belief can have a powerful effect on an athletic experience. In medical terms, the Masters Two-Step study is an example of the "negative placebo effect:" The man *believed* that he was going to get anginal pains on the forty-fourth count of the athletic exercise—and sure enough, he *did* get the pains. If he believed he had reached the forty-fourth count, he would experience the pains, even if the actual count was different.

This illustration has important implications for life-changing, positive personal fitness transformations. Just as this man's mind was conditioned in a negative way to develop pain, so *your* mind can be transformed in *positive* ways to help you achieve fitness.

Let's see how this can work through the application of the Principle of the Maximum Mind in three major fitness areas: establishing new fitness disciplines; enhancing your enjoyment of your current fitness activity; and improving your athletic performance.

### *Establishing a New Fitness Discipline*

For most people, especially after they reach their adult years, it's not easy to get started on a new fitness program. We tend to become comfortable in our more sedentary ways. It's very difficult to break old habits and begin new ones, especially when the new endeavors may involve the pain of sore muscles or other physical discomforts.

The first thing to keep in mind if you're planning a new exercise or fitness regimen is that it will probably take about a month for you to achieve meaningful results. That much transition time is usually necessary to establish new patterns of thought in your brain which will lead to new fitness habits for the future. Also, it usually takes about two to three weeks for the average sedentary adult to begin to get over the initial soreness that comes from exercising relatively unused muscles.

In general, most people who want to develop their

cardiovascular fitness will rely on the so-called aerobic endurance activities such as walking, running, jogging, cycling, swimming and perhaps cross-country skiing. In most cases, an individual will choose one of these activities and then concentrate on it until his or her fitness level improves significantly. Walking and jogging, which require relatively little skill and minimal equipment, tend to be two of the most popular of these activities.

Employing the Principle of the Maximum Mind during this transition phase, as well as beyond it, can make a big difference in your efforts to make the new athletic discipline or new fitness habit remain part of your behavior.

How does the Principle of the Maximum Mind work when you're trying to establish a new fitness discipline?

As usual, Phase One involves first eliciting the Relaxation Response. This will open you up to the possibilities of making better use of the right hemisphere of your brain. Any unhelpful left-hemisphere inferences—such as, "I'm constitutionally incapable of becoming an athlete"—can be transformed more easily when your brain is prepared in this way.

Next, in Phase Two, you should immediately begin to influence your left hemisphere with beneficial information, instructions and images. These should promote the changes you want and move you in the direction of your desired fitness discipline. In effect, during Phase Two you'll be creating new left-hemisphere inferences which should renew your mind and help transform your life.

Sometimes, something approximating this two-phase sequence can occur even when an individual knows nothing about the Principle of the Maximum Mind. I'm reminded of the experience of Barbara, an advertising executive in her early thirties, who started a swimming program long before the current popularity of fitness programs. She was a reasonably good swimmer when she began. But that wouldn't have been enough to keep her going if she hadn't immediately seen a connection between the repetitive activity of the swimming and her own need to find relief from her high-powered advertising work.

Barbara, who had just turned thirty, had been "feeling her age," as she said. She had been putting on weight, and in general she felt out of condition, tense and rather listless. Although she had never been involved in any formal athletics, she had sometimes enjoyed swimming. So she decided to join the local Y and see if there was any chance she could get into better condition.

This would-be swimmer knew nothing about the Principle of the Maximum Mind. For that matter, she knew nothing about the Relaxation Response. She really had no self-help philosophy of any kind to aid her as she began to develop this exercise discipline. Most likely, if her initial times in the pool had been uncomfortable or uninteresting for her, she would have dropped the activity.

In fact Barbara had a history of turning away abruptly from athletic endeavors if they didn't satisfy her immediately. She had started out playing tennis, but then had quit immediately. She had found she was getting hotter and perspiring more than she liked, and besides, she couldn't play well enough to keep the ball going for any length of time. Then, she had tried to increase the amount of time she spent walking. But on the hard city streets where she tried to exercise, she developed pain in her feet and knees.

Swimming turned out to be something quite different, primarily because she more or less came upon a highly positive experience that utilized the Principle of the Maximum Mind. Initially, there were some difficulties with swimming as there had been with other sports. For one thing, she could complete only about six laps in the Olympic-sized pool where she swam. The muscles in her legs and arms grew too tired to continue beyond that point. Also, she lacked the endurance to continue for much greater distances. Even with these physical difficulties, Barbara enjoyed swimming immensely, and she was exposed inadvertently to Phase One of the Principle of the Maximum Mind.

"The thing I really liked about swimming from the very beginning was that the water was so soothing," she explained. "Also, there was something about the rhythmic moving of arms and legs that lulled me into a kind of state I can't quite explain. But I do know that it was quite enjoyable and relaxing."

Here we have an example of that ineffable, right-brain experience that comes with the elicitation of the Relaxation Response and the introduction of the Principle of the Maximum Mind. The feelings became even more compelling as Barbara became more expert at her sport. She said that after she had been swimming for two or three weeks, the number of laps that she could do had doubled and then tripled. Gradually her mind began to focus primarily on the lap she was swimming.

In particular, every time her left arm entered the water during the first lap, she would say to herself "one . . . one . . . one . . ." Then, she would repeat the process when she was on the second lap, saying "two" every time her left arm entered the water.

Without being aware of what she was doing, this young woman was using as a meditative focus the number of the lap she happened to be on. That focus, repeated over and over again, combined with the rhythmic movement of her body to elicit the Relaxation Response.

Before long, after about three or four weeks, Barbara found that she would periodically tend to "merge" with the water. She felt almost as though she were becoming one with the waves that were flowing smoothly past her. Several other swimmers in the pool also mentioned having this experience, and this helped reinforce Barbara's expectations. More and more, she began to anticipate this new, exciting level of consciousness.

Barbara also got other forms of reinforcement from other swimmers she befriended at the pool. For one thing, after she swam, she often engaged in shop talk with other swimmers who were waiting to do their laps. They would discuss swimming techniques, equipment such as goggles and ear plugs, and the joy and satisfaction that they derived from their sport.

These conversations tended to bolster this young woman's commitment to her activity. As she put it, "I felt as though I had become a member of a great new club."

Once again, without knowing it, she was employing the Principle of the Maximum Mind: First, she elicited the Relaxation Response in the pool. Then, she concentrated on positive information and concepts related to the skills that she wanted to develop.

Barbara never had any problem wanting to leave her new discipline. This was rather remarkable, since she went through a period when there was some muscle soreness. Also, the workout sessions generally took at least an hour to an hour and a half for her to complete, from the time she left her office or home until she returned.

What we have here, then, is a significant commitment to a new skill which was greatly facilitated by the operation of the Principle of the Maximum Mind. Barbara's negative left-hemisphere inferences about exercise changed dramatically. It was only later that we were able to define what had probably enabled her to successfully begin and maintain this fitness discipline. She has now been swimming three to four times a week for about sixteen years.

What can you learn from this woman's experience, as well as from that of others who have finally managed to embark on a new fitness discipline?

Obviously, Barbara was motivated. She felt that she was losing her original youthful appearance. Like most of us, she had encountered a lot of difficulty in embarking on an exercise program. It was only after she picked a sport which she could pursue in the context of the Principle of the Maximum Mind that she finally succeeded.

Your goal, likewise, should be to use the basic two-phase approach to employing the Principle of the Maximum Mind. In other words, elicit the Relaxation Response first; then, focus on information and concepts which tend to reinforce the discipline which you want to begin.

There are limits to the new fitness disciplines which can be established through the Principle of the Maximum Mind. For example, the weight-reduction aspects of fitness may take considerable effort. With diets, a major problem is what has been called the "yo-yo" effect. This is the tendency of a person to lose weight and then to gain it right back; then, you lose it once more, only to gain it back again.

On the other hand, if reducing anxiety is an important factor in the ability to lose weight, relying on the Principle of the Maximum Mind can be very helpful and give long-lasting results—at long last. Anxiety or worry may contribute significantly to your tendency to overeat. Yet through the Principle you can reduce anxiety and remove a major contributing factor to your overeating.

The intransigence of weight problems and similar fitness challenges, however, usually requires something more. Among other things, it helps for your program to be firmly embedded in support networks. For example, you might participate in a group with members who also have your problem. If you have a sound belief system to help you, you're much more likely to succeed in these difficult areas.

One forty-year-old man, Allen, wanted to lose about fifteen pounds. This was not a great deal of excess weight for him, but enough to give him an unsightly roll of fat around his waist and to make him feel less positive about himself. No matter how much he tried, he couldn't lose weight. The only way he knew he was going to succeed was to cut down on the amount of food he was eating. Yet this had proven to be nearly impossible for him because of his love for sweets and desserts.

Allen didn't have the time or inclination to get involved in a special weight-reduction support group. He did have a deep personal religious faith. Not only did he sense strongly that *he* wanted to get the weight off, but also he believed firmly that God wanted him to get rid of it.

Unlike Barbara the swimmer, Allen was very much aware of how the Principle of the Maximum Mind could work. So he began to elicit the Relaxation Response during his morning prayer times. Immediately following this meditation period, he would focus on a passage of Scripture which he believed reinforced the idea that he should get that weight off. In particular, he liked these:

> . . . do you not know that your body is a temple of the Holy Spirit who is in you . . .?
>
> I Corinthians 6:19 (NASB)

> . . . present yourselves to God as those alive from the dead, and your members as instruments of righteousness to God.
>
> Romans 6:13 (NASB)

In this man's view, his failure to lose weight was an affront to God. Consequently, because he believed it was extremely important for him to conform to his own religious principles and scruples, he was highly motivated to take the weight off. He even brought the concern up at a regular prayer and discussion group he attended, and fellow believers there encouraged him in his resolve. By combining his periods of prayer and meditation with a focused consideration of specific passages of Scripture, Allen succeeded in losing fifteen pounds in several months.

As I've said, weight problems are extremely difficult to deal with, and Allen's situation was no exception, even with his strong faith and the reinforcement he received from fellow believers. During the next two months, he gained back five pounds.

After that, however, his weight remained stable. He found that he was able to avoid enough of the sweets and other fattening foods to keep his weight at a level only five pounds above his desired weight. He could even lose an extra pound now and then, as he concentrated anew on his use of the Principle of the Maximum Mind.

As we'll see later in our consideration of the use of the Principle of the Maximum Mind with spiritual disciplines, the relationship between changes in the brain and religious faith is very difficult if not impossible to describe scientifically. We hypothesize that what happened with Allen, as well as with many others who have succeeded with the Principle of the Maximum Mind, was that his brain became wired for new thought patterns and actions. He developed new left-hemisphere inferences about his eating habits. No one can measure the spiritual ingredient in this process, even though the force of this man's faith obviously was an important ingredient in his weight-loss achievement.

I would encourage anyone to employ the Principle of the Maximum Mind with physical fitness challenges, including weight-loss efforts. But be aware that you may need something extra to develop and support your belief system, such as a strong support group. In other words, a strong similar-interest or spiritual community may be necessary if you hope to succeed in the stubborn areas.

### *Enchancing Your Enjoyment of Fitness Programs*

Even after you've progressed with a new fitness regimen, you can still revert to sedentary ways. For one thing, you may suffer an injury and have to stay away from your athletic activity for a time, causing you to lose your exercise habit. Or you may get bored with the activity and decide that you really need to get away from it for a while or try something else. In such cases, you may very well be laying the groundwork for losing the discipline that you've established.

What can you do to incorporate your new discipline in your life so that you're unlikely to lose it?

One of the best "insurance policies" you can take out on your new discipline is to find ways to enhance your enjoyment of it. In the previous section, we saw how one woman swimmer began to experience an almost mystical sense of merging with the water. That was the swimmer's equivalent of the "runner's high" you may have heard about or experienced. In most endurance activities which require a regular, repetitive movement of the body's limbs, it's usually possible to undergo this quasi-transcendent or "high" experience.

As I've already indicated, this mystical type of athletic experience involves the elicitation of the Relaxation Response. A key factor is that the repetition of your physical movements continues as you run, swim or cycle over relatively long periods of time. The cadence carries your mind beyond the humdrum concerns of daily life to a more transcendent, altered state of consciousness. Once you've experienced this special mental state, in which we believe the right and left hemispheres are interacting differently, it will be enjoyable enough that you will strive to experience it again. That can provide an extremely powerful motivation to return to an aerobic activity, even if you've had to leave it for a period of time.

I recall one case of a man named Harold who had always hated to run. He had been forced to do road work of about two or three miles a day while he was engaged in athletic activities both in high school and college. He had also had to run for fairly long distances during basic training in the Marine Corps. Still, Harold never learned to like running or jogging.

As he embarked on a civilian business career, he made several attempts to begin a jogging program. He knew that he needed some sort of regular endurance conditioning to help him keep in condition. But after two or three unsuccessful attempts to get started, he finally gave up.

Then when the jogging craze began to gain momentum during the late 1970s, Harold read about the experience of the runner's high. The concept fascinated him because he had never experienced anything like this during the relatively short, anxiety-ridden exercising of his youth. When he was younger, he had always expected the running to be distasteful.

Harold found himself approaching this athletic activity with a different attitude. In addition to reading popular books on the subject, he became thoroughly immersed in the periodical literature of runners' magazines. Finally, he decided to give the sport another try. This time, the experience was completely different for him.

From his extensive reading, Harold knew that he had to expect to go through a period of two or three weeks to get his body into condition and his endurance capacities up to par. So he resolved to stay with his running program for at least a month. Soon, he found that he was experiencing the same fitness development that he had read about. By the end of the first month, the soreness had gone from his muscles and he could run three to four miles or even longer without getting out of breath.

Note what was happening here: This man combined extensive reading and study of the subject with the repetitive aspects of his jogging. These factors, along with his increasing sense of well-being from physical activity, helped him develop an intense belief that running would work for him. He continued to read and study the subject as he pursued his running program. He also found that he was thinking about many of the basic exercise concepts as he was engaging in his workouts.

The Principle of the Maximum Mind was clearly at work. Harold was in a position to elicit the Relaxation Response constantly through the regular repetition of his footfalls as he ran over a distance of several miles. He also focused before, during and after his runs on positive, exercise-related ideas and information. In short, he was changing the way his brain was structured. New brain pathways were enabling him to develop new, positive habits about fitness. He was supplanting old, negative left-hemisphere inferences with newer, more positive ones.

Before long, Harold experienced the runner's high—the analog to the merging phenomenon which the female swimmer had reported. These experiences don't happen during every workout. They may come only sporadically. But the exhilarating feeling occurs often enough to make the amateur athlete continue to seek it time and time again.

In this man's case, the first time he experienced the runner's high was when he passed the four-mile mark on one of his runs. "Up to that point, I knew that I was the one providing the energy for the run," Harold recalled. "I wasn't having any particular trouble, and my energy levels were fine. Still, I was the one who was in control of the movements of my body.

"Then, all of a sudden, I sensed that I was *being pulled* along. The running took absolutely no effort on my part. I felt as though I could go on forever. I also had a sense of oneness with the trees and water about me. I really became very excited and happy—exuberant would be the best word. I kept on going, about six or seven miles that day, and I didn't even want to stop at that point."

It was fortunate for Harold's conditioning program that he had this experience when he did because a week or so later he sustained a serious injury in a weekend basketball game. He tore ligaments in his left ankle and had to walk around on crutches and endure an uncomfortable cast for about a month. Of course, he was unable to continue with his running regimen during this time.

Many times, when such accidents occur, the enforced break from exercise causes an individual to lose the habit that he has worked so hard to develop. In Harold's case, he desperately wanted to get back to his running program again. The day after he took the cast off, he was out walking in anticipation of strengthening his injured ankle and returning to his former level of conditioning. Interestingly, he experienced almost no muscle soreness when he began some light jogging again about ten days later. One of the major factors that was driving him back to his fitness program was the tantalizing memory of that high that he had experienced weeks before.

For most joggers, the preliminary period of conditioning can be relatively short: It usually doesn't take a great deal of skill to run. So a period of three to four weeks is often sufficient to establish the discipline and to position a person to experience the runner's high. In any event, repetition and a passive, "let it happen" attitude are important, both to develop skills and to enhance the chances of having the high experience. If the high is your goal, you must avoid trying to force any euphoria to occur. It should happen if you'll just let it happen.

### *Improving Your Athletic Performance*

As you spend more time with your chosen fitness program, it's possible that you'll begin to develop an interest in the competitive aspects of your sport. You may want to try your skills against others in various meets and tournaments. That will provide an excellent opportunity to apply the Principle of the Maximum Mind to your athletic endeavors.

On a very simple level, the Relaxation Response has been shown by controlled studies to improve the reflex time in normal individuals. In one 1980 study, the fourteen people who were tested for the responses of their reflexes were able to decrease their total reflex time by 14.41 milliseconds after five weeks of twice a day elicitations of the Relaxation Response.

Professional athletes, as well as serious amateurs, have become more aware in recent years of the mental dimensions of superior athletic achievement. Various top sports figures have enrolled in courses which teach them how to visualize the perfect game, play or stroke. This conceptual approach, which is another application of the Principle of the Maximum Mind, enables them to achieve higher levels of focus and concentration when they're engaging in competitive activity. The end result can be a significant improvement in performance.

One effective procedure involves first eliciting the Relaxation Response. Then, the athlete forms a mental picture or image of what the perfect or ideal athletic expression or achievement would be. Using such an approach, top-level athletes can often achieve a significant degree of inner serenity and preparedness before a match or game. Finally, through various relaxation, visualization or imaging techniques, they may be able to maintain that inner sense of balance throughout much of the athletic encounter.

Some of the best examples of these performance-enhancing techniques can be found in tennis and other racquet sports. Racquet sports require an exceptional level of skill development and training, so much so that even a slight variation in the execution of certain strokes among top players may mean the difference between losing and winning. It's been said that at least half and maybe as much as 80 percent of tennis is mental.

One instructive exercise is to observe two of the "mentally tough" champions, Chris Evert Lloyd and Ivan Lendl, as they perform on the court. Lloyd and Lendl are particularly good examples because as you study them when the television cameras zoom in on their faces, they often seem to be in a world of their own. Neither appears to be particularly affected by outside distractions or influences. Both appear to be in a near-meditative state.

In tennis parlance, a game played at a high level of winning expertise is often said to be played "in the zone." As explained in an article in the *New York Times** the "zone" involves a mental state "so complete and intense that it evokes a state of almost semiconscious euphoria—one that many believe bears a resemblance to hypnosis, and enables a top player to achieve his or her peak performance."

This state is characterized by psychologists as an altered mental state, which involves a tremendous sense of happiness, timelessness, effortlessness and positive thinking. Usually, those who are playing in the zone actually expect to win.

"I've had matches in the last couple of years where everything has gone right," Chris Evert Lloyd told a *New York Times* reporter.** "You play in the zone, over your head where everything is like a dream. When you play matches like that, you want to play more."

Here we have a case of the euphoric high that

* September 5, 1986
** September 4, 1986

runners, swimmers and other conditioned athletes have experienced—but with a difference. In this case, the euphoria is a key factor in a winning performance, not just an enjoyable athletic by-product. The Principle of the Maximum Mind is clearly at work here, as the players achieve a transcendent state of mind which produces a superior expression of their great athletic skills.

When they are in this state, the athletes' well-honed skills "play out" as they had previously been wired in their brains through visualization and practice sessions. Their training in the use of a passive attitude is also quite important: This state of mind allows athletes to passively disregard worries and inferences that would produce "performance anxiety" and impede performance.

Nonprofessional athletes have similar experiences. One squash player, after playing about four times a week for a couple of years, developed his skills to a level where he could sustain long rallies with excellent opponents. On his best days, he would report a sense of "flowing" about on the court.

"It almost seems as though I could do no wrong," he said. "My opponent would hit the ball at very difficult angles, but somehow I would always seem to be there. I knew instinctively where his next shot was going to go. It was almost as though someone or something outside of me was moving me about, with a minimum expenditure of energy. When I came off the court on one of those days, I felt as though I was floating around on a cloud for the next hour or so."

In such cases, a prerequisite to the high or transcendent experience is a relatively advanced level of conditioning and expertise. You have to make a commitment to get into condition. You also need to develop a sufficiently advanced level of athletic skills to make sustained performance possible.

A closely related way that the Principle can work with racquet-sport enthusiasts is through other visualization techniques in the training process. Geoffrey C. Harvey, a teaching tennis professional at the Badminton and Tennis Club in Boston, trains his tennis students to elicit the Relaxation Response as they are learning to stroke the ball. Then they visualize an idealized stroke through videotapes and mime. In this way, the tennis players imprint their minds with the ideal concept and action for each stroke.

What's the point of this? Harvey realizes that the player's mind can be better utilized in the training process and that the mind is also the most important enemy of good performance. His objectives are to first "program" the mind and then get the mind—specifically, the left hemisphere of the brain, with all its anxieties and negative inferences and expectations—out of the way and let the body "do its own thing."

One weekend player, Marsha, tried this type of technique and found that the approach helped her improve her game markedly against one of her most difficult opponents. Marsha, who was in her mid-forties, had found that she was stuck at a certain playing level with this opponent. Typically she could win only one or two games at the most in each set from the other woman. Many times, the internal scores of the games were quite close, but somehow, Marsha managed to lose most of them. Her opponent usually controlled the play so that Marsha found herself scrambling about, always playing defensively, just trying to return the shots that the other woman placed so well.

Then Marsha decided to start using a meditation and visualization technique, much like the one recommended by Geoffrey Harvey. On the first occasion, before she went out on the court, she spent a few minutes at home eliciting the Relaxation Response through meditation. Then, she imagined what the game she was about to play would be like. In her mind's eye, she saw herself moving back and forth on the court, anticipating her opponent's best shots and seizing the initiative to place her own shots out of reach. When she finally reached the tennis courts, she continued to meditate both before and after each shot that she made.

"The results really were amazing," she said. "Instead of always losing the games, I found that I was actually pushing this gal at the end of the first set. We were tied five all in games—the first time I had ever done this well against her. She finally won that set, but I could see that our competition would no longer be the same."

It's particularly interesting that this was Marsha's first attempt at using the Principle of the Maximum Mind on the tennis court. Yet in her first session, she experienced dramatic improvement in her play. She was able to get her brain's left hemisphere, with its anxieties, doubts and questions, out of the way most of the time and just allow her body to flow back and forth on the court. At times, she actually felt that she knew where the ball was going before her opponent even hit it. Of course, there were also times when her meditative techniques lapsed, and she reverted to her old style of play. But she had sensed such a distinct difference when she was meditating on the court that she immediately returned to the maximum-mind mode.

Although the change in Marsha's tennis-playing habits began almost immediately, many times it takes days and sometimes even weeks to see significant progress. Ultimately, if you stay with it, the Principle of the Maximum Mind should raise your level of play noticeably in almost any sport.

Sam, a serious amateur squash player, also took a giant step forward in his game as a result of a similar technique. He had developed some hard, low crosscourt and "rail" shots which enabled him to best many opponents who were not too quick on their feet. Against those who were more agile and who had developed their skills to about his level, he found that his game lacked sufficient variety to make him a consistent winner.

So Sam bought a simple, basic book on squash techniques, *Sports Illustrated Squash*, by the editors of *Sports Illustrated*. One of the shots which interested him in this volume was the "boast for nick from backcourt," a rather difficult maneuver which requires the player to hit a hard, glancing shot off the back side wall. From there, the squash ball is supposed to hit the front wall in the corner and then "nick" the front side wall for a winner.

Sam first went through his regular meditation session to elicit the Relaxation Response. Immediately afterward, he read and studied the diagrams and description of this particular shot. He also imagined himself on the court, hitting the boast for nick against a couple of his toughest opponents. As he thought about it, he allowed himself to anticipate problems he might have in executing the shot. In effect, he actually played through about a dozen squash points in his mind, each of them ending in this difficult new maneuver that he wanted to master.

The next day, when he stepped onto the squash court, Sam continued to meditate periodically, and he recalled to his mind's eye the way that he wanted to hit that boast for nick. As a result, when the opportunity arose to try it, he was primed for the attempt. A difficult, well-placed shot came back to him in the back court, and he whipped his squash racquet around at the ball and fired it into the side wall nearest to him.

"It was incredible," he said. "The ball angled right up to the opposite corner at the front wall and then dribbled down against the bottom of the front side wall for a winner. It happened just like the diagrams in the book had pictured it."

Of course Sam didn't always hit this shot perfectly. It's far too difficult for an intermediate-level amateur to achieve absolute consistency with a stroke like this. But from the very beginning he did hit a high percentage of winners. He also developed a reputation as a person whose bag of tricks on the squash court was something to be reckoned with.

Such uses of the Principle of the Maximum Mind are by no means limited to racquet sports, however. Freeman McNeil, the running back for the New York Jets football team, said in the *Boston Globe** that he relies

* September 10, 1986.

on a practice called "endodynamics," which he says is a kind of mystical blend of positive thinking and physical responses.

"Basically, the concept is that of mind and body," McNeil told a reporter. "Whatever you see, you correlate it with your body. I'll be running off pure instinct, and my body will be following whatever my subconscious mind sees at the time."

Sometimes, he says, when he runs a particular play, he moves through it without thinking logically or analytically about what he's doing.

"It'll be like thumbing back into my [mind's] files and just copying it," he says. "It's just a feeling now where I don't even hesitate. I just go."

Experiences like these are difficult to put into words. We already know the reason for this: McNeil and other athletes who are utilizing these techniques are dealing largely with experiences rooted in the right hemisphere of the brain—experiences which, by definition, can't easily be put into words. Like the tennis and squash players we've considered, NcNeil seems to just "get his mind out of the way." He lets his bodily movements flow under the influence of the brain's right hemisphere. The more he does this, the more he "grooves" those patterns of thinking and acting in his brain—and the more his mind is conditioned to operate smoothly and efficiently in the new, more productive modes.

This approach seems to work in baseball as well. Boston Red Sox pitcher Bruce Hurst, who starred in the 1986 World Series, has attended the Sports Enhancement Association in Naples, Florida. This institute, which strives to build confidence in athletes, is reportedly the source of a great deal of Hurst's success.

"They teach you imagery and focusing on what you have to do," Hurst said. "It's like what John Wooden used to preach when he told his players to lie down and visualize the ball going through the hoop. And whatever John Wooden says is good enough for me."*

In all these situations, the process of mental transformation seems to be substantially the same. That is, the Principle of the Maximum Mind is at work. First, the person gets into a relaxed, meditative mode which elicits the Relaxation Response, with its distinctive physiological features. Then, the athlete visualizes, studies or otherwise focuses on the changes which he wants to occur in his mind and playing habits.

Dr. Armand M. Nicholi, a psychiatrist with the Harvard Medical School, began working with professional football players of the New England Patriots in 1982. As he reported in the *New England Journal of Medicine*, he contacted me, discussed our research with the Relaxation Response and, finally, devised "a method of preparing the team for competition that several players say has helped to improve their play."

Specifically, a player may rehearse a particular play in his mind and then find himself executing the play successfully in a game. For example, the last game of the 1985–86 season against the Cincinnati Bengals was one that had to be won if the Patriots were to enter the play-offs. With less than two minutes to go, a substitute running back entered the game and ran a play exactly as he had been visualizing it—and he scored the winning touchdown!

A recent Harvard study by Dr. Stephen M. Kosslyn

* *New York Daily News*, October 27, 1986

and his associates of how people form and use mental images indicated that everyone can have some type of mental image. A small percentage of people are superb at it. More than 80 percent of mental images occur in color; about 40 percent involve movement; and about 10 percent consist of images that fade in and out. The uses for the images include decision-making, understanding verbal descriptions, changing one's feelings, self-motivation and training for peak athletic performance.

It's my impression that even though most of us have the capacity to use imaging techniques to improve ourselves, we don't use this ability as much as we might. The Principle of the Maximum Mind, especially as it's applied to athletic performance, offers a tremendous opportunity to develop and fine-tune these visualization abilities—as well as to improve our fitness levels significantly.

Now let's explore some practical ways of improving your fitness. We've seen how many other people in a variety of circumstances have established new fitness disciplines, enhanced their enjoyment of athletic activity and improved their performance significantly. It's time for you to try to experience some of these same benefits.

Take a good look at yourself and decide where you need to improve your fitness level or athletic skills. (First, if you suffer from any ailment or are over thirty-five, have your physician examine you and get his or her approval.) If you're a completely sedentary person, you might do well to get started on some sort of mild or moderate exercise program. Or if you're already in reasonably good condition, you could possibly use an extra dose of enjoyment from your athletic activity. Finally, if you're deeply involved in tennis, swimming, cycling or some other sport on a competitive basis, you may be interested in improving your performance.

In any event, settle on a goal and then begin to make beneficial changes in your mind and in your life. Discuss your proposed course of action with your maximum mind guide. As we've done before, we'll first focus on eliciting the Relaxation Response in Phase One of the Principle of the Maximum Mind. Then, we'll move on to Phase Two—focusing the left hemisphere of your brain on key discipline-shaping information and concepts which will help you establish new pathways in your brain for your new skills.

### *Phase One*

**Step 1:** Pick a focus word or short phrase that's firmly rooted in your personal belief system. As we've already seen, a Christian person might choose the opening words of Psalm 23, "The Lord is my shepherd"; a Jewish person, "Shalom"; a nonreligious individual, a neutral word like "one" or "peace."

**Step 2:** Sit quietly in a comfortable position.

**Step 3:** Close your eyes—*unless* you're eliciting the Relaxation Response as you're exercising. For a technique to use during exercise, see below.

**Step 4:** Relax your muscles.

**Step 5:** Breathe slowly and naturally and, as you do, repeat your focus word or phrase as you exhale.

**Step 6:** Assume a passive attitude. Don't worry about how well you're doing. When other thoughts come to mind, simply say to yourself, "Oh, well," and gently return to the repetition.

**Step 7:** Continue for ten to twenty minutes.

**Step 8:** Practice the technique once or twice daily.

*Alternate Phase One: For Use During Exercise*

**Step 1:** If you're over thirty-five or if you suffer from a physical ailment, first obtain your physician's advice.

**Step 2:** Get into good condition. This means being able to exercise without becoming short of breath or suffering muscle fatigue for at least thirty minutes of endurance activity (such as jogging, walking or swimming). Or you should be able to exercise continuously for a comparable length of time while participating in another sport.

**Step 3:** Do your usual warm-up exercises.

**Step 4:** As you exercise, keep your eyes open.

**Step 5:** Become aware of your breathing. Focus your attention on the in-and-out rhythm of your breath.

**Step 6:** Where it's comfortable during the regular cadence of your breathing or footfalls, repeat your focus word or phrase.

**Step 7:** Maintain a passive attitude. Don't worry about how well you're doing. When other thoughts come to mind, simply say to yourself, "Oh, well," and gently return to your regular breathing and focus word.

**Step 8:** When you've completed your exercise session, use a low-intensity cool-down routine to bring your body's metabolism back to normal.

### *Phase Two*

After you've elicited the Relaxation Response, spend ten to twenty minutes looking over some of the following thoughts and passages. See which ones apply best to the changes which you want to experience inside yourself.

You may very well find that, given your particular interests, you should go to other sources to find relevant words and thoughts to focus upon. Or, you may simply want to visualize the desired skill or the perfect game. Don't hesitate to ask the advice of someone whom you trust and who shares your belief system. Now, here are a few passages to get you started thinking.

> Do you not know that you are a temple of God, and that the Holy Spirit of God dwells in you? If any man destroys the temple of God, God will destroy him, for the temple of God is holy, and that is what you are.
>
> I Corinthians 3:16-17 (NASB)

> In order that people may be happy in their work, these three things are needed: They must be fit for it: They must not do too much of it: And they must have a sense of success in it.
>
> John Ruskin,
> *Pre-Raphaelitism*

> This is the law of the Yukon, that only the strong shall thrive;
> That surely the Weak shall perish, and only the Fit survive.
>
> Robert William Service,
> *The Law of the Yukon*

Oh it is excellent to have a giant's strength; but it is tyrannous to use it like a giant.

William Shakespeare,
*Measure for Measure*

. . . strength is felt from hope . . .

Homer, *Iliad*

My strength is the strength of ten,
Because my heart is pure.

Alfred, Lord Tennyson,
*Sir Galahad*

The Lord is my strength and song and he has become my salvation.

Exodus 15:2 (KJV)

They that wait upon the Lord shall renew their strength; they shall mount up with wings as eagles; they shall run, and not be weary; and they shall walk, and not faint.

Isaiah 40:31 (KJV)

I believe that man will not merely endure: he will prevail.

William Faulkner,
speech on receiving the Nobel Prize
in Stockholm, December 10, 1950

To endure is greater than to dare; to tire out hostile fortune; to be daunted by no difficulty; to keep heart when all have lost it; to go through intrigue spotless; to forego even ambition when the end is gained—who can say this is not greatness?

William Makepeace Thackeray,
*The Virginians*

. . . if the young swimmer can be taught to believe in himself and have confidence in his abilities . . . physiologically there is no limit to what he can do. The drawbacks are psychological; lack of sufficient confidence.

. . . if enough inspiration is given the . . . swimmer and he is endowed with enough imagination, all things being equal, there is no limit to the results he can achieve.

. . . the more mileage covered by a swimmer through the years, year in and year out, the greater the chances for success, especially in middle-distance swimming. There is no easy road nor shortcut to organic strength and vigor. This constitutional power can only be built as in the case of kmuscular power, by intelligent application of work, work, training and work, *ad infinitum*. This is the sort of conditioning that cannot be bought in pill-form over the counter. Athletic achievement and success, like all good things in life, can only be bought through hard work, sacrifice and discipline.

R.J.H. Kiphuth,
*Swimming*

*Why You Should Be Fit*

Research has shown that:

The physically fit person is able to withstand fatigue for longer periods than the unfit;

The physically fit person is better equipped to tolerate physical stress;

The physically fit person has a stronger and more efficient heart; and

There is a relationship between good physical alertness, absence of nervous tension, and physical fitness.

*Royal Canadian Air Force*
*Exercise Plans for Physical Fitness*

One of the great principles of the universe is the principle of balance. . . . To function properly, every part of our world, no matter how minuscule, must be in a state of complete equilibrium.

And so it is with our bodies.

The human body is just another part of the universe that is meant to be in perfect balance. We have been constructed in such a way that we need just so much exercise, no more and no less. We need just so much food of certain types. And we need just the right amount of sleep and relief from the tensions and stresses of life. . . . Where there is balance, there is a sense of well-being.

Aerobic exercises refer to those activities that require oxygen for prolonged periods and place such demands on the body that it is required to improve its capacity to handle oxygen. As a result of aerobic exercise, there are beneficial changes that occur in the lungs, the heart and the vascular system. . . .

But at the heart of any effective aerobic exercise program is the principle of balance. . . . Recent research has shown that unless a person is training for marathons or other competitive events, it's best to limit running to around 12 to 15 miles per week. More than that will greatly increase the incidence of joint and bone injuries and other ailments; on the other hand, less mileage will fail to achieve the desired improvement in the body.

If you run more than 15 miles per week, you are running for something other than fitness and the emotional balance, good health and good looks that accompany it.

Dr. Kenneth H. Cooper,
*The Aerobics Program for Total Well Being*

Most of the people I talked with told me they thought they benefited psychologically from running. This did not surprise me, for I myself have long known that I have. Some of the benefits, as already indicated, are easily described: a sense of enhanced mental energy and concentration, a feeling of heightened mental acuity. (You don't necessarily notice these things every day, or after every run. But most of the time they're there.) Because our everyday language is not often called upon to describe such phenomena, other benefits are more difficult to put into words.

Once you have been running for a few months, you invariably notice some remarkable psychological dividends—a feeling of calmness and power, of being in control of your life. Runners also speak of having an "addiction" . . . and in a sense they unquestionably do. It is rare to meet a runner, no

> matter how busy, who considers giving up his sport. More often, the contrary is true; someone who runs three or four miles a day—plenty for fitness alone—will in time inexplicably double or even triple his mileage.
>
> James F. Fixx,
> *The Complete Book of Running*

> Between 30 and 40 minutes [after beginning aerobic exercise] some people experience the "opening up" phenomenon. They begin to breathe more freely, their chest lifts and the entire system seems to work more at ease. It's a powerful, wonderful feeling. It's akin to waking something up inside you.
>
> [At] 30 to 45 minutes into the run . . . the first of the possible alterations in consciousness begins to occur. These alterations are usually sensory. The senses seem to increase in alertness. All of them respond: sight, hearing, touch, taste, smell and position.
>
> Thaddeus Kostrubala,
> *The Joy of Running*

As I've mentioned, these are just a few possibilities for you to focus on as you embark on your mind-changing fitness program. You may find that after a period of prayer and meditation, you want to spend a considerable amount of time reading about the sport or exercise program that interests you. That's certainly a good way to help rewire the pathways in your brain which are related to fitness and exercise. To this end, you might pick up one of the reliable, popular exercise books which can be found in your local bookstore or library. The main idea is just first to open your mind up with the Relaxation Response. Then, you expose yourself to materials which will help your brain begin to undergo beneficial changes.

A fit body is only part of the story of a well-balanced, satisfied life, however. Most of us are at least as interested in improving our mental performance, including the acquisition of new intellectual skills and the fine-tuning of old ones. The Principle of the Maximum Mind can be a powerful force in helping us achieve these objectives.

# 7.

# *The Secret to Improving Your Brain Power*

Practically everybody wants to make better use of his or her mind. That may mean improving learning ability, problem-solving skills, creativity or a variety of other intellectually based capacities.

How many of us have embarked on the study of a foreign language, only to lose interest or get distracted after a few lessons? How many continue trying to make decisions and solve problems at work in old ways, even though we realize we're not as efficient as we might be? How many face a new challenge with the common response, "I just can't seem to come up with any new ideas"?

A problem underlying many intellectual dead ends and mental roadblocks is that our thought patterns are often locked into inefficient ways of tackling issues. We need new insights and novel approaches. Yet how do we break free of our own intellectual restraints? An answer lies in applying the Principle of the Maximum Mind.

To understand how you can enjoy an increase in intellectual discipline and overall "brain power," let me share three representative examples from my own clinical experience. They focus on improvement in academic classwork, in writing efforts and in daily efficiency on the job.

### *Enhancing Your Brain Power in Academic Endeavors*

Kathy, a woman in her mid-forties, had a very busy and frenetic life, both as a full-time professional career woman and as the mother of five children. She wanted more. She wished to return to school to acquire an advanced degree which she felt would make her more marketable and would also provide her with greater personal satisfaction.

Kathy also felt she was under far too much pressure. She didn't think she was handling the stresses in her life very well, certainly not well enough to undertake a major new educational venture and career change.

Her problems were compounded when she was diagnosed as having moderately high blood pressure. As a result, her physicians placed her on standard medications for hypertension. Her blood pressure decreased somewhat, but the drugs still didn't reduce it to normal levels. Kathy was also bothered by some of the side effects produced by the medication, including feelings of fatigue and an inability to concentrate. She often observed, "I just don't feel very good."

Because she knew that stress could play a part in hypertension, she contacted us to see if we could do anything about relieving her condition without the aid of drugs. That seemed to her to be a solution for achieving a better control of her life and her academic objectives.

She came to her initial visit well prepared: She had already read one of my books, and she was convinced that the Relaxation Response could help her break the cycle of anxiety and stress which was contributing to her blood-pressure problem.

"The change in me did not occur overnight," Kathy reported later. "It's taken time and a great deal of self-discipline. I was taught the Relaxation Response during my first visit, and I also joined a hypertension program at the hospital, which added diet and exercise to my daily agenda."

From her present perspective, however, the central factor in her improvement has been the use of the Relaxation Response every morning and night. "I no longer feel as if time is constantly yelping at my heels, causing anxiety," Kathy said. "I don't experience the spurts of adrenaline, the constricting blood vessels and the inevitable rise in my blood pressure. Instead, my sense of calmness has grown, and gradually my blood pressure has become normal."

Interestingly, her life soon become *more* demanding, rather than less. During her Relaxation Response therapy, she made the strategic decision to shift her career focus—a change which can produce extra stress in anyone—she embarked on a course of study as a full-time graduate student.

As a result of inner transformations that she was

experiencing, she was different. She successfully completed the requirements of her academic work and soon passed her qualifying exams. In addition to the academic pressures, Kathy maintained a half-time job and also continued with the rigors—and, as she emphasizes, "the joys"—of her family life.

"As I approach my fiftieth year, I feel vigorous, and I have a strong sense of well-being," Kathy concludes. "There is a genuine calmness within me now. I have discovered a way to soothe myself during those times of high stress. I believe it's a way which has always been there inside me, but which has lain dormant and unknown throughout much of my adult life. The use of the Relaxation Response has in effect given me the power to improve my health and therefore to enhance my life."

Kathy provides an instructive example of how the Principle of the Maximum Mind can enhance a person's ability to stay tranquil in the face of major daily pressures—and at the same time promote success in a new academic endeavor. Kathy didn't really eliminate any of the items on her busy schedule. She merely shifted direction and took on new responsibilities, which required her to "stretch" and test her mind in a demanding university setting.

How can we explain what happened to her thinking mechanisms during this experience?

First of all, she opened the door to beneficial change and reduced counterproductive learning-inhibiting anxieties by eliciting the Relaxation Response on a regular basis. In other words, she utilized Phase One of the Principle of the Maximum Mind. Then, she made use of Phase Two by staying in regular touch with us at the medical center, where we helped reinforce her resolve to move in this new direction in her life. Also, and perhaps most important, she attended an established university and involved herself in academic life. At the university, she enjoyed regular encounters with like-minded teachers and students.

As for this last point, let me emphasize that getting involved in a formal classroom situation, especially one which requires examinations and leads to a formal degree, will help reinforce your efforts to develop a new academic discipline. Trying to pursue a new academic enterprise on your own, such as by learning a new language through records and tapes, is a more difficult course.

If you do choose a more individual, isolated approach to learning, it's important to develop some reinforcing influences to help you stay on the right track. You might acquire a maximum mind guide, such as a tutor or other expert in the discipline you've chosen. Or you should otherwise expose yourself to people, literature or concepts which will help condition you during Phase Two.

### *Developing Discipline in Writing*

Many people experience writer's block at one time or another. It happens when an aspiring executive is assigned a major report which he knows will be decisive in his future career. It also happens with those who have to prepare minutes of meetings, presentations for fund-raising efforts or speeches designed to promote a cause. In such cases, you know the words have to be put on the blank sheet of paper sitting in front of you;

but somehow, you just can't get them out of your head and into print.

Something akin to this happened with James, a young man in his late twenties, who couldn't finish his doctoral dissertation at a major university. When he came to us for treatment about three years ago, his major concern was that his high blood pressure was not responding properly to drug therapy. In his conversations with me, he said he felt his anxiety arose from a deep fear that he might be repeating a problem that had plagued his father: a serious heart disease which had taken the older man's life only a couple of years before.

An additional problem this man faced was that he became especially anxious when he had to have a medical examination: That experience tended to elevate his blood pressure even further. As a result, he was caught in a cycle of steadily increasing blood pressure readings, even as he was taking increasing doses of drugs, such as the so-called diuretics and beta-blocking agents.

"My fear was crippling," he said. "I was lonely and yet not dealing with this loneliness. My work performance was uninspired. And I was making little progress on my dissertation."

This man's condition offered an excellent opportunity for the application of the Principle of the Maximum Mind. First of all, we taught him a simple technique of meditation, which has been described several times in this book as Phase One of the Principle. James had a solid background in Catholicism, and he was eager to try to recapture some of the vitality of his faith, which he felt he had lost in recent years. So he chose a simple prayer as the key words in his meditation. This approach worked almost immediately. Within a few weeks, his blood pressure readings were normal, and he no longer needed medication.

"My religion has always been important to me, but daily prayer had no longer been a part of my life," he told me. "Although I had many years of formal Catholic education, I hadn't realized how comforting prayer could be. Meditation has helped me overcome my anxieties."

That was just the first step in the life-changing experience that James was undergoing. He also moved into Phase Two of the Principle of the Maximum Mind by exposing himself to several important influences which helped to change his patterns of thinking.

First, he went into psychotherapy. His therapist served as a kind of maximum mind guide who helped him deal with some of the problems in his research work, as well as in his stalled dissertation.

He married a supportive woman who constantly encouraged him in his work and ambitions.

And he stayed in touch with us at the medical center, as sort of secondary maximum mind guides. We helped reinforce the patterns of transformation which were beginning to take place in him.

The final result? James tells it best in his own words:

"I still have many fears, but I'm coping much better with them. This past year has been very rich for me. I've finished my dissertation and graduated in June. My wife and I have bought a charming old house, which we are renovating. Also, we are expecting a child this May. And I have found a more interesting and challenging research job, which I am now beginning. Many exciting things have happened for me. Finally, I am moving ahead again!"

This man's writing block was obviously part of a much broader problem. In any case, he first reduced the excessive anxieties and fears which had immobilized him. Then, he exposed himself to people and influences which helped promote internal thinking transformations. As a result, he succeeded in solving major problems in his life.

When you're confronted with a demanding task at work, including a very difficult writing project, a *little* pressure and stress can be a good thing. It can enhance your performance and whet your appetite for learning and achievement. Too much stress, however, can become a negative influence. In fact, as happened with James, the pressure may get so overwhelming that it can completely immobilize you.

There's nothing new about this insight. Two Harvard researchers, Robert M. Yerkes and John D. Dodson, showed in the first part of this century that as stress and anxiety intensify, efficiency and levels of performance go up as well, but at a certain point of stress, efficiency and performance will begin to decline.

James, like many of us, first had to find a way to reduce the excess stress in his life. Only then could he undergo sufficient beneficial changes to overcome his writing block.

### *Achieving Calmness and Increased Efficiency on the Job*

Highly motivated people tend to be high achievers. You give them a job to do, and they'll approach it with

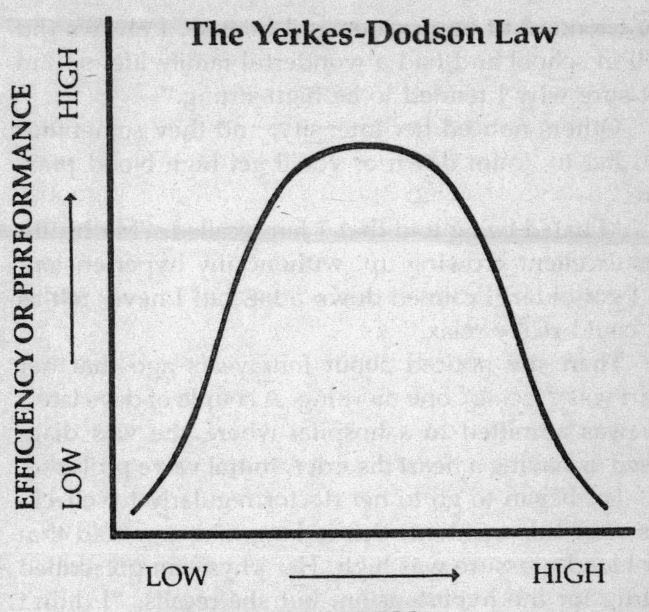


an enthusiasm and intensity that makes employers wish all their workers were like them.

Yet problems can develop with this approach. Intense people may have a great deal of trouble getting along with their fellow workers. Commonly, they don't enjoy themselves very much. They often feel dissatisfied with their own performance, with their bosses, and with their fellow workers. For whatever reason, their demands of themselves and others are in many cases far too high for the development of satisfying relationships.

Jan, a patient of mine in her mid-thirties, faced some of these problems. As she put it, "While growing up, I tended to be nervous and intense. I always did well in school and had a wonderful family life, so I'm not sure why I tended to be high-strung."

Others noticed her intensity, and they sometimes told her to "calm down or you'll get high blood pressure."

"I hated being told that," Jan recalled. "My health was excellent growing up, without any hypertension. As I got older, I calmed down a lot, but I never felt as if I could really relax."

Then she noticed about four years ago that her heart was "racing" one morning. A couple of days later, she was admitted to a hospital where she was diagnosed as having a heart disorder, mitral valve prolapse.

Jan began to go to her doctor regularly for checkups after this incident. Before long, she was told that her blood pressure was high. Her physician prescribed a drug for the hypertension, but she recalls, "I didn't feel any different or any calmer. And my blood pressure would still spike."

She became more anxious about the drugs she was taking, and her blood pressure gradually escalated. As a result, her medications were increased. She was caught in a vicious cycle that was, in a sense, a self-fulfilling prophecy.

To control her hypertension, she turned to some self-help techniques. First she joined a health club and began to exercise regularly, but without any improvement in the blood pressure. She began preparing all her food from a no-salt cookbook. This attempt to control her diet very strictly didn't lower her blood pressure or alleviate her anxiety.

Finally, while describing her problem to a co-worker,

she learned about the possibility of using Relaxation Response techniques to control hypertension. Eventually, she came to our office. At her first visit, the years of having been told to "calm down" because her "blood pressure will get too high" had made her so sensitive she was embarrassed about even discussing the subject. She said, "I was convinced people would think less of me if they knew I took medication for high blood pressure."

Like James in our previous example, Jan was a person whose background involved deep religious faith. So it was easy for her to begin a meditation program by using a prayer, the Roman Catholics' Hail Mary, which was quite meaningful to her. Soon, her life began to change for the better.

"By repeating the prayer to myself, I found I could relax anytime during the day, including the times when I felt stress," she said.

Even when she wasn't trying to meditate, she reported beginning to experience "an increasingly deep feeling of calm" both on the job and also in her social encounters. In many ways, Jan has become the antithesis of the high-strung person that she used to be, and her work life has been a major beneficiary.

"If a stressful situation arises during daily life, I find that when the situation is over, I can return to a relaxed feeling very quickly," she explains. "I calm down during my half-hour lunch to a level that I could never attain before. I find that some silly things I used to react to—such as crazy drivers—don't rile me in the same way anymore."

In the past Jan had also been quite impatient—a characteristic that can make life unpleasant for oneself *and* one's business colleagues. She has now learned to accept the fact that life has a certain pace, with a variety of stops, starts and delays in everyone's daily schedule. That insight has flavored her relationships with others and her approach to her work.

"Impatience helped to get my blood pressure up where it was," she noted.

Now she requires no medication, and her blood pressure is consistently normal. Contrary to her own expectations, a change has occurred in her—a change which provides a powerful demonstration of the Principle of the Maximum Mind.

Jan admits frankly, "I was afraid meditation wouldn't work. I was desperate to make people believe I was calm. Yet all those feelings helped provide the fuel to push up the mercury sky high [in the blood-pressure measuring device]. When the meditation began to help in spite of my fears, I really began to believe in it as something that could work for me. Now I *know* that meditating—saying Hail Mary—calms me and puts me at peace within myself."

Jan, like many others, opened the door for change with her prayer-meditations. That brought her through Phase One of the Principle of the Maximum Mind. Then, she exposed herself regularly to mind-changing influences, especially the encouragement and instruction that she received in our offices. As a result, Phase Two of the Principle became effective in her life. Soon, important changes began to occur.

Jan had doubted that this approach would work for her because she had tried so many other methods and had failed with them. Yet despite her reservations, a transformation took place. The power of the Principle of the Maximum Mind actually began to work even when she seemed to lack the conviction that change could occur in her life.

Could this be an example of how sometimes belief may not be necessary in the working of the Principle? In fact, the most important kind of belief *was* present in Jan's experience, because she pursued her meditation in the context of her deepest personal belief system. Her underlying religious faith, reflected in the prayer she chose, was very much at work, giving her a sense of assurance and positive expectation, even though she wasn't so sure about the specific Relaxation Response technique she was trying.

It really didn't make much difference whether or not she believed that some abstract, and to her, unproven, change would occur in her body and brain. The important point is that the change *did* occur, and it eventually arose out of the context of her deepest beliefs. As a result, Jan found herself in a position to be much happier and calmer. In the long run, she also became more efficient in her work, as well as more effective and pleasant in the other commitments in her life.

### *The Evidence for Intellectual Improvement*

From a scientific point of view, much more research needs to be done to establish the effectiveness of using Relaxation Response techniques, and also the Principle of the Maximum Mind, in enhancing intellectual endeavors. As time passes, the supporting evidence continues to accumulate in the clinical and research findings of various investigations.

For example, in a 1981 study conducted by Drs. M. S. Fiebert and T. M. Mead, students were placed on a program using meditation techniques, which had been designed to improve their attention and concentration skills. The ultimate objective was to study the students' learning abilities. The specific technique used was called actualism meditation. This method consists of a set of techniques intended to help people direct their attention, increase their awareness of reality, and also channel their sources of mental and physical energy.

The students, after being taught the actualism techniques, were asked to practice them before they studied and before their examinations. A control group of students also used the meditation exercises, but they were asked to practice them at times *other* than those involving studying or exams.

As you can see, the experimental group's program was set up to test the usefulness of the Principle of the Maximum Mind: One group of students first elicited the Relaxation Response. Then, immediately afterwards, they exposed their minds to the academic information and exercises related to the improvement of their learning and performance. The other students in the control group, by not "plugging in" the Phase Two part of the Principle of the Maximum Mind immediately after Phase One, were less susceptible to the operation of the Principle.

The final results? The experimental group, who had in effect utilized the Principle of the Maximum Mind, showed a significant increase in their examination grades, as compared with the control group. The researchers noted that the results of the study couldn't be attributed to differences in study time because the two groups devoted about the same amount of time to their preparation.

In another study, which is a doctoral thesis of Dr. A. I. Abrams, a group of elementary school children were taught a variety of meditation, contemplation or concentration techniques. Their academic performance was then compared with a control group, which was not taught any of the techniques. In the end, the students who used the meditation, concentration and relaxation techniques showed a higher level of academic achievement on standard achievement tests. Also, they demonstrated higher levels of cognitive growth, as measured by a series of psychological measuring scales.

In this study, we can again see how the Principle of the Maximum Mind may have been at work. The students' minds were first opened during the meditative phase. Their thought patterns were then rewired during the classroom teaching and exercises which followed the meditation. The students in the experimental group also tended to become calmer through the elicitation of the Relaxation Response. This increased calmness undoubtedly tended to reduce their levels of anxiety and agitation, and thus made them better prepared to learn new skills and information.

Psychological studies also suggest that the Principle of the Maximum Mind can be quite effective in increasing the effectiveness of business problem-solving. A group of management graduate students, with no previous meditation or relaxation technique experience, were taught certain meditation and relaxation techniques by Dr. H. S. Kindler as part of his doctoral thesis. Another group, a control group against whom the others were being tested, simply listened to taped lectures on problem solving or on meditation.

The researcher found that the people who were using the meditation techniques were able to solve group problems faster, and with fewer transactions among themselves, than the control group. The meditation technique group also reported feeling less tense and experiencing more effective teamwork than did the control group.

Now, consider what could have been happening in the thinking patterns of these management students. First, the group that used the Relaxation Response techniques opened their minds to beneficial change by eliciting the Relaxation Response. This was Phase One of the Principle of the Maximum Mind. This experience not only prepared them for a personal transformation, but also reduced their anxiety levels and enhanced their abilities to relate effectively to other people.

Then they moved into Phase Two of the Principle of the Maximum Mind with their participation in the group problem solving. In this stage, their thinking processes could operate more freely and efficiently to reach answers to the difficult management decisions that faced them.

Not all psychological studies have upheld the idea that the use of Relaxation Response techniques, such as meditation, prayer or contemplation methods, will improve one's intellectual abilities. In fact, several studies have come to the conclusion that the use of these techniques makes no difference.

When you analyze these negative studies, however, it appears that the researchers and participants applied only the first phase of the Principle of the Maximum Mind. That is, an individual or group might elicit the Relaxation Response and thereby reduce anxiety and enjoy various other psychological and physical benefits. But the participants don't achieve the altered patterns of thinking brought on by the second phase; they lack planned exposure to the influence of information, people or concepts that will direct the mind toward the desired changes.

The weight of the research evidence is moving us closer to a more complete knowledge of the power of the Principle of the Maximum Mind in enhancing our brain power. We still don't fully understand all of the practical techniques and methods needed to hone our maximum mind powers, but progress is being made.

Before we move on to the practical exercises which you'll use to enhance your brain power, there are several considerations or tips you may want to keep in mind. These should prove to be of practical value as you try to establish new intellectual disciplines and improve your own abilities at problem solving and creativity.

**Tip #1: Don't forget your maximum mind guide.** In intellectual areas, as much as any other, you'll need a person or group to meet with on a regular basis for encouragement, guidance and instruction. I'm reminded here of some observations by a neurologist at the University of California Medical Center, Dr. Frank R. Wilson, who contends that every human being, even those of advanced years, can be a musician.*

Dr. Wilson, who began to play the piano when he was forty years old, says that he believes that everyone

* *The New York Times*, July 13, 1986

is actually *meant* to be a musician. Furthermore, by playing an instrument, an individual can help refine and develop his brain and neuromuscular system.

"You can't look at the human brain without saying this is the brain of an organism designed to interact with its environment in a musical way," he told a reporter.

Among other things, he says, the human brain provides for refined movements of the arm and hand muscles for playing instruments. Certain parts of the brain have become highly specialized in sound analysis and processing—abilities which, he argues, are important for musicians.

So why aren't we all strumming harps, playing pipes and otherwise making beautiful music? One of the biggest roadblocks that we face, Dr. Wilson says, is that "many music teachers don't know how to teach music at all." They can teach people who are already fairly advanced musically. But they don't know what to do with a beginner. In other words, he argues that we have a lack of adequate maximum mind directors in the musical field.

Dr. Wilson even highlights the beneficial changes which can take place under the right guidance with a person who is involved in an effective music program. He says that the brain may actually change as people heighten their abilities with music and that there are indications the transformations may actually help slow the aging process.

**Tip #2: Make up your mind to enjoy, rather than worry about, the learning process.** Dr. Wilson has also found during his own middle-aged piano-playing practice that it's essential to stop worrying about impressing others and just to enjoy the process.

"Nobody ever tells people that practicing is fun," he says. "Coming home from work and fiddling around at the keyboard or the banjo is inherently enjoyable."

This approach to learning and personal improvement reflects a *passivity* that can help you get immersed in the learning process without the impediments of anxiety which so often hold you back from establishing and pursuing a new intellectual discipline. Many times, when we just let go and allow ourselves to enjoy the learning experience, we begin to take steps forward in our new abilities.

One middle-aged man, who had just taken up playing the cello, echoes this sentiment: "I can feel like I'm at a plateau and progressing very slowly. And then all of a sudden I realize that something has changed in my playing. It's very subtle and creeps up very slowly, and then it stares me in the face, and I feel tremendously satisfied."

As you'll recall, an essential part of eliciting the Relaxation Response involves staying passive. When extraneous thoughts intrude, say to yourself, "Oh, well." Then, you turn back to the concept, prayer or phrase upon which you're meditating. This same passivity should carry over into the learning process—and it *will* carry over if you'll apply the Principle of the Maximum Mind in proper order, first with Phase One and then with Phase Two.

In practicing the piano, for instance, you might first elicit the Relaxation Response through your chosen meditative or prayer technique. Then, when you've finished with this first phase of the Principle of the Maximum Mind, you move on to Phase Two: You condition or influence your mind in the desired direction. With piano playing, that can simply be by playing the piano. In other words, you sit down after you've elicited the Relaxation Response and begin your practicing. Or, you might go into an instruction session with your music teacher (your maximum mind guide). Or, on some occasions, you might do some reading in the musical area.

If you follow this approach, the chances are enhanced that you'll have the same kind of enjoyable experiences to report as did the amateur pianist Dr. Robert Wilson or the novice cellist.

**Tip #3: Don't underestimate the negative power of stress.** Throughout this entire discussion, we've frequently mentioned the negative effects of excessive stress or anxiety. These destructive forces can undercut your attempts to establish a new learning discipline or pursue an approach to effective problem solving or creativity. The sources of stress are pervasive.

A recent Lewis-Harris survey indicated that health problems caused by stress, rather than by physical illness, are causing a large amount of absenteeism at work. In this particular study, one-fourth of those interviewed reported that they had stress-related problems. Half of the people with stress problems had been forced to restrict their daily work routines.

The national Centers for Disease Control (CDC) confirmed this trend by concluding recently that stress and boredom in the workplace cause substantial health problems—and the situation may well get worse. People are particularly bothered by such things as too much work, lack of control over their jobs, unsupportive bosses and co-workers, and restrictions on opportunities at work. The CDC noted further that these stressful conditions on the job can result in neuroses, depression, anxiety, irritability, drug abuse, problems with sleep and a variety of physical ailments such as stomach pains and headaches.

In a similar vein, Kenneth R. Pelletier of the University of California, San Francisco, has noted in his book *Healthy People in Unhealthy Places*: "Although the stereotype of the harried business executive is the most common image which comes to mind in discussing workplace stress, every worker grapples with it. According to a national survey published by Blue Cross, five out of six workers at all levels of employment indicated stress as a major factor in their occupations resulting in 'dissatisfaction, low self-esteem, angina, persistent coughs, and neurotic behavior.' "

If you find yourself subjected to excessive pressures on a daily basis, you're not in a very good position to learn new things or enhance your brain power. One of your first objectives should be to change your situatiion to make it less stressful. Sometimes this is quite difficult or even impossible. If this is the case, you can at least learn to protect yourself against the harmful effects of stress.

As we've already seen in a number of examples in this book, one of the best techniques for reducing the harmful effects of stress is the elicitation of the Relaxation Response, or Phase One of the Principle of the Maximum Mind. Then, with this newfound capacity to adjust to your situation, you can experience Phase Two.

**Tip #4: Experiment with creativity.** Creativity is a

very difficult concept to define because it means different things to different people. For some, being creative means coming up with ideas. For others, you're only truly creative if there is a practical dimension to your novel concepts or strategies.

Then there's the issue of the relationship between creativity and originality. Some people believe that to be creative, you must be original: The idea, concept or approach you come up with must be entirely new. Others would say that it's not necessary to be original—just to put old things or ideas together in new ways. As the preacher says in Ecclesiastes, "What has been is what will be, and what has been done is what will be done; and there is nothing new under the sun."

Creativity means different things in different fields. For a business person, creativity may mean the ability to solve financial problems that perplex most other people. In advertising, the creative person is one who can capture the essence of the best sales pitch for a product or service in just the right words or pictures.

Because it's so difficult to define creativity, social scientists have been confronted with great problems in studying it. In the popular press, this difficulty is reflected in such headlines as "Science Grapples with the Creative Puzzle," which appeared in *The New York Times* on May 13, 1984.

In this particular *Times* article, the author, Dr. Howard Gardner, a researcher in psychology at Boston Veterans' Hospital and co-director of the Harvard Project Zero, describes the wide variety of definitions and understandings of creativity. Gardner assumes that for a person to be "creative"—or to engage in original, significant work—he must first spend a considerable amount of time developing the skills necessary to accomplish such work. Furthermore, he says, there are "multiple intelligences" among human beings. For example, some people have a special ability and creativity with words, others with numbers, others with spatial information, others with music, and so forth. Each of these "intelligences," in Gardner's view, "undergoes a particular developmental history and each has a separate representation in the human brain."

Other researchers into this murky area of creativity emphasize the importance of allowing the brain to work subconsciously on a problem. Some even stress the importance of dreams in coming up with new ideas or concepts which most people would classify as creative.

A business application of "whole brain thinking"—or a coherence between the right and left hemispheres of the brain—has been orchestrated by Norman W. Brown, a Harvard M.B.A. graduate and chief executive of the advertising firm Foote, Cone & Belding Communications, Inc. When he assumed office in 1982, Brown immediately classified the company's account executives as "left brains" and the creative people as "right brains." Most important of all, he urged them to recognize one another's strengths and to try to work together more closely in coming up with advertising programs.

One of the reasons that Brown decided to emphasize getting his left-brain and right-brain people working together more closely is that he noticed many "great ideas were being wasted" in the company.

How is his creativity campaign progressing?

The reputation of his firm for coming up with bright new advertising concepts has been improving. Many observers, for example, were impressed with a Foote ad promoting Sara Lee bagels: A woman was shown enjoying a bagel sensually to the accompaniment of "bump-and-grind music," as *Business Week* put it. This, of course, was the right-hemisphere contingent in the company holding sway. In another commercial for Coor's beer, an actor took a more analytical approach by discussing the high quality and natural ingredients of the drink. Here, the left-hemisphere representatives made a few points.

One message that comes across in such illustrations is that the term "creativity" is not something which can be easily defined. Perhaps the difficulty in describing and understanding the concept can be traced to its right-hemispheric origins. As we've already seen, it's the left hemisphere of the brain which controls speech, inferences and logical analysis. Yet those qualities may be only a part, and indeed, a small part, of the total creativity inherent in a person's mind.

It's not always so easy, then, to discover what creativity means and how it should be expressed in your life. It's necessary therefore for you to *experiment* frequently with the Principle of the Maximum Mind as you try to increase your own creativity. Furthermore, you'll usually find that you must first develop certain basic skills—that is, create necessary brain wirings—before you can even begin to experiment. It's rather difficult to be a creative writer, for instance, if you don't have some experiences putting words together into coherent sentences. It's impossible to be a creative scientist if you don't have the basic knowledge of the scientific discipline in which you want to be creative.

All this may seem painfully obvious. Yet it's surprising how many people think creativity is somehow a quality which sits off by itself in a person's mind or personality, just waiting to be used, regardless of any prior preparation, study or experience.

Even when you finally have the requisite skills to be creative, there's still not always a direct line to the creative idea or solution. Many times, you have to approach things frontways, sideways or even through the rear door of your mind in order to achieve a level of creativity which is usable.

This brings up another situation in which the Principle of the Maximum Mind is useful. First, you enter Phase One by eliciting the Relaxation Response. Then, in Phase Two, you begin to expose yourself to the subject matter with which you want to have a creative impact. You may have to experiment at this point. Instead of tackling your primary issue head-on, you'll need to wait, or back off for a time.

Here's how this might work: If you're facing a difficult problem at work, you might first elicit the Relaxation Response in Phase One. Then, leave the office and get completely away from the business issues you're trying to resolve. By backing off in this way, you're more likely to encounter the creative mental "light bulb" which is going to give you the answer. Specifically, you may need to go out jogging; or take a walk and do some window shopping; or browse through the books at your local bookstore; or go out for coffee with some colleague and start chatting about something. With all these approaches, the problem or issue which requires your creativity will recede from the "front-burner" of your mind. That may be just what is needed. For the right hemisphere of your brain to have sufficient freedom and encouragement to spark creativity, you may have to distract the left hemisphere from focusing analytically on the subject in question.

Ultimately this approach will likely make you more creative. You'll probably also find it's very difficult to quantify or define exactly what factors have caused the breakthroughs that you're experiencing in your work or avocations. Again, the reason for this is that the right hemisphere of your brain must be integrally involved in creative thought—we can't put the operations of the right hemisphere readily into words.

### *How to Enhance Your Brain Power*

Now, let's turn to the practical steps of improving your brain power. First, decide what it is you want to do to enhance your intellectual abilities: learn a new skill, solve problems more efficiently, or increase your creativity, for example. When you have your objective firmly in mind, move on to an application of the Principle of the Maximum Mind. Once again, here is a description of Phase One and Phase Two.

### *Phase One*

**Step 1:** Pick a focus word or short phrase that's firmly rooted in your personal belief system. As we've already seen, a Christian person might choose the opening words of Psalm 23, "The Lord is my shepherd"; a Jewish person, "Shalom"; a nonreligious individual, a neutral word like "one" or "peace."

**Step 2:** Sit quietly in a comfortable position.

**Step 3:** Close your eyes.

**Step 4:** Relax your muscles.

**Step 5:** Breathe slowly and naturally and, as you do, repeat your focus word or phrase as you exhale.

**Step 6:** Assume a pasive attitude. Don't worry about how well you're doing. When other thoughts come to mind, simply say to yourself, "Oh, well," and gently return to the repetition.

**Step 7:** Continue for ten to twenty minutes.

**Step 8:** Practice the technique once or twice daily.

### *Phase Two*

Now that you have opened your mind through the elicitation of the Relaxation Response, it's time to expose yourself for at least fifteen or twenty minutes to important influences which will help "renew" your mind along the intellectual paths that you have chosen. You may already have some specific information, study material or images which you want to focus on. You may, at this juncture, simply wish to back off for a while and allow your own innate creative capabilities to take hold. Or if you would like some more general concepts to think about, try a few of those which follow.

Devise, wit; write, pen; for I am for whole volumes in folio.

Shakespeare,
*Love's Labour's Lost*

For where is any author in the world
Teaches such beauty as a woman's eye?
Learning is but an adjunct to ourself.

Shakespeare,
*Love Labour's Lost*

. . . I have fears that I may cease to be
Before my pen has glean'd my teeming brain.
John Keats,
"When I Have Fears"

Where my heart lies, let my brain lie also.
Robert Browning,
*Men and Women, One Word More*

Oh, their Rafael of the dear Madonnas,
Oh, their Dante of the dread Inferno,
Wrote one song—and in my brain I sing it,
Drew one angel—borne, see, on my bosom!
Robert Browning,
*Men and Women, One Word More*

But if the great sun move not of himself; but is as an errand-boy in heaven; nor one single star can revolve, but by some invisible power; how then can this one small heart beat; this one small brain think thoughts; unless God does that beating, does that thinking, does that living, and not I. By heaven, man, we are turned round and round in this world, like yonder windlass, and Fate is the handspike.

Thinking is, or ought to be, a coolness and a calmness; and our poor hearts throb, and our poor brains beat too much for that.
Herman Melville,
*Moby Dick*

Of all the causes which conspire to blind
Man's erring judgment, and misguide the mind,

What the weak head with strongest bias rules,
Is pride, the never-failing vice of fools.

A little learning is a dangerous thing;
Drink deep, or taste not the Pierian spring:
There shallow draughts intoxicate the brain,
And drinking largely sobers us again.

Alexander Pope,
"Essay on Criticism"

With curious art the brain, too finely wrought,
Preys on herself, and is destroyed by thought.

Charles Churchill,
"Epistle to William Hogarth"

Let knowledge grow from more to more,
But more of reverence in us dwell;
That mind and soul, according well,
May make one music as before.

Alfred, Lord Tennyson,
"In Memoriam"

No man ever forgot the visitations of that power to his heart and brain, which created all things new; which was the dawn in him of music, poetry, and art.

Ralph Waldo Emerson,
*Essays: First Series, Love*

Life is too short to waste
In critic peep or cynic bark,
Quarrel or reprimand:
'Twill soon be dark;

Up! mind thine own aim, and
God speed the mark!

Ralph Waldo Emerson,
*Poems*

Education is the instruction of the intellect in the laws of Nature, under which name I include not merely things and their forces, but men and their ways; and the fashioning of the affections and of the will into an earnest and loving desire to move in harmony with those laws.

For every man the world is as fresh as it was at the first day, and as full of untold novelties for him who has the eyes to see them.

T. H. Huxley,
*A Liberal Education*

Indeed he knows not how to know who
knows not also how to un-know.

Sir Richard Francis Burton,
*The Kasidah of Haji Abdu El-Yazdi*, VI, 18

Intellect is to emotion as our clothes are to our bodies: we could not very well have civilized life without clothes, but we would be in a poor way if we had only clothes without bodies.

Alfred North Whitehead,
*Dialogues of Alfred North Whitehead*

Thought is the labour of the intellect, reverie is its pleasure.

Victor Hugo,
*Les Misérables*

Books are not absolutely dead things, but do contain a potency of life in them to be as active as that soul was whose progeny they are; nay they do preserve as in a vial the purest efficacy and extraction of that living intellect that bred them.

John Milton, *Areopagitica*

It is of no small benefit on finding oneself in bed in the dark to go over again in the imagination the main outlines of the forms previously studied, or of other noteworthy things conceived by ingenious speculation.

Leonardo da Vinci,
*Note-books*

The object Truth, or the satisfaction of the intellect, and the object Passion, or the excitement of the heart, are, although attainable, to a certain extent, in poetry, far more readily attainable in prose.

Edgar Allan Poe,
*The Philosophy of Composition*

Simplicity of character is no hindrance to subtlety of intellect.

John, Viscount Morley,
*Life of Gladstone*

While there is one untrodden tract
For intellect or will,
And men are free to think and act,
Life is worth living still.

Alfred Austin,
*Is Life Worth Living?*

So long as a man imagines that he cannot do this or that, so long is he determined not to do it: and consequently, so long it is impossible to him that he should do it.

Benedict (Baruch) Spinoza,
*Ethics*

Wisdom will repudiate thee, if thou think to enquire WHY things are as they are or whence they came: thy task is first to learn WHAT IS, and in pursuant knowledge pure intellect will find pure pleasure and the only ground for a philosophy comformable to truth.

Robert Bridges,
*The Testament of Beauty*

There are three classes of intellects: one which comprehends by itself; another which appreciates what others comprehend; and a third which neither comprehends by itself nor by the showing of others; the first is the most excellent, the second is good, the third is useless.

Where the willingness is great, the difficulties cannot be great.

Niccolò Machiavelli,
*The Prince*

A quotation, a chance word heard in an unexpected quarter, puts me on the trail of the book destined to achieve some intellectual advancement in me.

George Moore,
*Confessions of a Young Man*

Two things that in my opinion reinforce one another and remain eternally true are: Do not quench your inspiration and imagination, do not become the slave of your model; and again: Take the model and study it, otherwise your inspiration will never become plastically concrete.

Vincent van Gogh,
Letter to Theo van Gogh

The most beautiful thing we can experience is the mysterious. It is the source of all true art and science.

Albert Einstein,
"What I Believe"

# 8.

## *The Spiritual Side*

Personal belief, and often traditional religious concepts, have been deeply involved in much of what we've presented so far in this book.

For example, the focus word which you've been encouraged to use during your meditations should be rooted in the Faith Factor, or your most dearly held personal belief system. This connection with your personal beliefs will frequently involve religious conviction. Whatever the source of the belief, deep personal conviction of some sort is very helpful in inducing the full impact of Phase One of the Principle of the Maximum Mind—which, of course, involves the elicitation of the Relaxation Response.

Also, many times, spiritual growth is a by-product of other personal progress. It's a fact that people who improve their health, frame of mind, physical fitness or intellectual capacities may simultaneouly experience a broadening and deepening of their personal value system and world view.

In light of this, it won't be surprising if you want to apply the Principle of the Maximum Mind directly to your spiritual development. But here, we're treading on very sensitive ground. If we had difficulty defining "creative" in the previous chapter, we face many more problems in defining "spiritual."

It could be easy to misinterpret what we're trying to do in our attempt to relate the Principle of the Maximum Mind to spiritual matters. Too often, when self-help and mind-control advocates begin to wax eloquent in promoting their own particular cause, the tail may begin to wag the dog from a spiritual viewpoint. That is, these schemes may actually threaten to supplant or subvert more traditional answers to the meaning of life than effectively augment them.

Let me state at the outset that it's *not* my purpose to try to provide an alternative to traditional religion or spirituality. On the contrary, as far as I'm concerned, traditional religion and spirituality should be the basic control mechanisms to keep self-help methods and other personal improvement programs in proper perspective.

My main objective in this chapter, and in other sections of the book as well, is to describe an important human capacity, the Maximum Mind, which can be used not only for mundane forms of self-improvement, but also for the enhancement of faith. In fact, many people who have moved to deeper levels in their personal philosophies and religious traditions are already using this particular meditative approach. All I can do or them is to explain, to the extent I believe scientific :nowledge and words allow, part of what is happening n their minds and bodies as they pray and meditate ınd begin to see significant changes occur in them- elves.

Neither are my explanations an attempt to explain ıway spirituality. I believe that the ultimate sources of pirituality could come from outside a person and may ıever be susceptible to physical or chemical analysis. n short, my main purpose is to try to elucidate some of the scientific implications for phenomena which reach ar beyond science as we know it.

Even though this is scientifically sensitive and even langerous ground, I feel compelled to try to find a easonable path through this rich, mysterious and often reacherous maze. Spirituality is not just a part of life. Defined in the broadest sense, it's the very foundation of life.

Since the earliest annals of recorded history, hu- nan beings have been engaging in an ongoing search or the meaning of life and death. In the ancient *Epic of Gilgamesh*—which is the story of the spiritual search of a king of an important city of ancient Sumer nearly 4,600 years ago—the protagonist Gilgamesh searches lesperately for the meaning of life. His friend, Enkidu, ıas died by an arbitrary decision of the gods. Gilgamesh eels he must know the meaning of his friend's death.

Try as he may, he can't solve the puzzle of life. Again and again, he is told that his search is fruitless. The final answer which comes to him—an answer which s devastating—is that there is no permanence in the ıniverse. Even knowing the worst, Gilgamesh is able o accept the undesirable news and return to his ordinary life with a sense of hope and a commitment to his goddess, Ishtar.

Deep, probing questions and enigmatic answers also emerge from the earliest parts of the Bible. The lives of Adam and Eve and their descendants are centered completely on how they relate to Yahweh, the faithful but demanding God who interacts constantly with them from their creation, through their fall, and on into their later acts of rebellion and obedience.

This same spiritual saga continues today, though sometimes in other forms. Certainly, modern-day Americans are a highly religious people: According to surveys by the Gallup poll over the last few decades, a consistently high proportion of our population, about 95 percent, say that they believe in God.

Why this broad-based spiritual orientation of humankind? For one thing, the left hemisphere of our brains has been able, apparently from the very beginning, to infer that we're going to die. We're perhaps the only creatures on earth who are able to recognize this eventuality. The next logical step, after we infer death, is to look for an antidote or answer to prevent despair. Many have found a solution in religious faith. Faith in God may help to make life tolerable, even in the face of death's certainty.

On the other hand, if religion is not a meaningful part of a person's life, he or she may turn instead to one of the self-help systems or personal improvement philosophies as a substitute. What motivates many of our fitness advocates or other self-improvement enthusiasts may be a desire, sometimes subconscious, to beat or put off death. In fact, many experts feel that underlying most of our anxieties, fears and phobias is the great fear of death. In his Pulitzer Prize–winning book *The Denial of Death*, Ernest Becker declared that death is "the basic fear that influences all others, a fear from which no one is immune, no matter how disguised it may be."

In recent years, there has been considerable speculation about how the spiritual side of our lives may relate to the structure of our brains.

One theory, propounded by Julian Jaynes, a research psychologist at Princeton University, is that man's brain changed into a bicameral structure, with the left hemisphere focusing on speech and analysis, and the right hemisphere producing the "inner commands." In an early stage of man's evolution, the innate "inner voices" began to break through into the mind via the right hemisphere of the brain. These voices were accepted as a kind of "divine command," to direct people to take certain action. Jaynes saw the voices as an outgrowth of developing language abilities, personal volition and responses to stressful situations which required different decisions.

In Jaynes' view, although humans began to use language around 100,000 B.C., they had neither the abilities nor the will to exercise reflection, or a broad understanding of time until 10,000 B.C. The "inner voices," a product of the right hemisphere of the brain, helped to guide the actions of people in those early days. Eventually, the voices were assumed to be divine. This development, according to Jaynes, helped give rise to all religions.

As Jaynes sees it, there was no "consciousness"

in Homer's *Iliad*, in the sense that "the heroes do not wonder, ponder or decide. They are pulled around by the voices of the gods."

Likewise, the patriarch Abraham isn't "conscious" in the Bible because of the same characteristics. Jaynes believes that consciousness, in the sense that he is defining it, comes later, with the wisdom literature, including *Ecclesiastes*.

Do these voices survive today? Jaynes' answer: Only in hallucinations of the type that schizophrenics may experience, or perhaps in intense mystical states.

Another more biologically bound view is propounded by Dr. Arnold Mandell, a brain chemist and professor of psychiatry at the University of California in San Diego. In Mandell's view, there may be an inherent neurochemical mechanism which can explain spiritual and transcendental experiences of consciousness.

Specifically, Mandell believes that deep prayer and meditation, fasting and extensive endurance exercises, such as marathon running, may stop the action of the neurotransmitter serotonin. The blocking of serotonin, which usually tends to calm the brain down, also helps intensify electrical activity in the parts of the brain that control spatial concepts, movement perception and also emotions. The final result, as Mandell puts it, is "affectual and cognitive processes characteristic of religious ecstasy and the permanent personality changes associated with religious conversion."

Others have attempted to integrate the workings of the brain into theological categories. Dr. James B. Ashbrook, a professor of religion and personality at Garrett-Evangelical Theological Seminary in Evanston,

Illinois, believes that the inexplicable workings of the brain—which he defines as "mind"—connect the brain to the "realm of transcendent meaning.

"The brain does not—and cannot—contain the cosmos," Ashbrook declares. "No physiological process adequately accounts for human purposing. Belief patterns, however, do articulate a cosmos; they do order and organize what matters in and to human life."

As Ashbrook sees it, the analytical and language-oriented workings of the left hemisphere of the brain are related to what is known in religion as "proclamation" This involves a verbal statement of what is true and an urging of one's hearers to act. In contrast, what Ashbrook calls "manifestation" involves "eliciting wonder and participation apart from formal language." Manifestation, as he sees it, is "incapable of being articulated, and more experienced than expressed." In short, we have here a classic right-hemispheric channel for religious expression.

• • •

My own view is that the spiritual side of our experience cannot be explained only in terms of physiological or biological processes. To be sure, spiritual experiences may be accompanied by physical responses which may be measured by scientific instruments. But I don't believe that you can explain the underlying bases of these experiences by "hard" medical science, as it is now largely defined.

Hard medical science requires that "reducibility" be present. This means it's necessary to reduce the causes of a disease to their specific underlying biochemical or physiological bases. The disease can then be treated with a drug or a procedure that reverses the basic cause. For example, pneumonia is often caused by invading bacteria. If you kill the invaders with penicillin, you cure the disease.

When a disease cannot be defined or "framed" in such reductionistic terms, its study and treatments are considered to be a lesser, "softer" science. Anxiety, for instance, a disorder related to the thinking processes, cannot be reduced to one physiological cause. The psychological assessments and treatments of anxiety are therefore called soft science.

The fact that such phenomena of the mind cannot be reduced beyond a certain level because of the incomprehensibly complex interactions of the brain doesn't mean that their effects do not exist. Indeed, they *do* exist and may result in measurable, reproducible and predictable changes. In other words, they meet basic criteria of scientific study. Such nonreductionistic events are not easily categorized in scientific terms or by some scientifically oriented minds. As William James once observed:

"If there is anything which human history demonstrates, it is the extreme slowness with which the ordinary academic and critical minds acknowledge facts . . . which present themselves as wild facts, with no stall or pigeonhole, or as facts which threaten to break up the accepted system."

When James refers to "the ordinary academic and critical minds," he's referring to minds with predominantly left-hemispheric functions. Reductionistic thinking is a left-hemispheric function because it's rooted in logic and subject to analysis and verbal description.

Spirituality, in contrast, is often a manifestation of

right-hemispheric functions which cannot be readily described in words. So it seems to me to be shortsighted to denigrate the scientific study of human phenomena such as spirituality simply because they do not fit a currently accepted framework.

In short, I wonder if perhaps those who most vigorously espouse only hard reductionistic medical science may be excessively wired into left-hemispheric thinking. As a result, they may have difficulty experiencing right-hemispheric concepts. It's akin to an adult's trying to explain physical love to a five-year-old. The youngster might recognize the adult is attempting to convey something important; but he has no developed capacity to understand fully what's being said.

In a sense, from a practical scientific viewpoint, the extent to which spiritual events occur within the workings of our brain or as separate entities beyond us doesn't matter. Either way, we are in a win-win situation.

On the one hand, if spiritual occurrences, including healing functions, have a brain-based dimension solely inside our heads and bodies, future researchers will find underutilized human capacities—which are available to be tapped through various self-help techniques and medical treatments. On the other hand, if our brains turn out to be "receivers" for powers, forces and energies that exist outside ourselves, we may never be able to perform a complete scientific analysis. The outside forces may still prove to be quite real, powerful and potentially beneficial for us.

Many of these points about the dangers of reductionistic scientific thinking have a bearing on our attitudes toward future research. There are also implications that have a direct application to the present. For one thing, the physical responses that go along with spiritual experience can now point us to a better understanding of that experience, and may even enhance the experience.

For example, I don't believe it's an accident that many modern-day worship services are structured so that the first part of the session involves music, meditation, prayer, and liturgy. Then, the final part of the service typically involves a "proclamation" through a sermon, homily or lecture. Finally, in some groups, particularly those with an evangelical orientation, the worship service may conclude with some sort of a call to action, such as an "altar call."

In terms of the Principle of the Maximum Mind, let's examine what's happening under these circumstances. In the first part of the service, steps that include prayer, meditation and liturgy are being taken which are likely to elicit the Relaxation Response—or Phase One of the Principle. This, of course, is an approach which emphasizes the use of the right hemisphere of the brain.

Then, as the congregants move toward the last part of the service, they are ready to hear the sermon, which is designed to influence their thinking and actions. In the first segment of the service they have been *prepared* for this later exhortation and mind-changing, life-changing experience. Finally, the minister, priest or rabbi may conclude with a strong flourish, such as a call to decision or action. In this case, the entire service will be "wrapped up" in the "proclamation" in a way that can involve a powerful application of the Principle of the Maximum Mind.

Unfortunately, as many church- and synagogue-goers will attest, the structure of services often falls far short of these ends. But when a service is organized appropriately—and when those who are participating are there out of a strong sense of belief and expectation—amazing transformations in lives can take place.

Even as I describe this sequence of events in a religious service, I'm wary of going too far. This analysis is *not* meant to be a mechanistic presentation of how a clergyperson can manipulate people's lives, apart from the operation of some divine, outside force or deity. Rather, it's just a way of pointing out that the "work of the spirit," if you will, can be greatly facilitated if those who plan services are aware of a possible master design underlying the workings of our minds.

Now, let's take a look at some concrete illustrations of how the spiritual side of certain individuals has been enhanced and transformed as a result of the Principle of the Maximum Mind. First of all, I'll describe some examples from my own experience:

**1. Meditative prayers can strengthen faith.** One woman, Roberta, has been a cardiac patient for nearly twenty years. She's suffered a series of minor heart attacks, incidents of congestive heart failure and severe attacks of angina pectoris. She has also been hospitalized for weeks on end and has had to miss work for two to three months at a time as a result of each of her heart problems.

When she came to us for help, her severe heart condition and also a problem with diabetes made it necessary to keep her on many medications. We introduced her to a Phase One technique which would enable her to elicit the Relaxation Response. For her faith-based focus phrase to be used in eliciting the Response, Roberta chose "Lord Jesus," though sometimes she would say, "Heavenly Father."

Roberta describes the impact of this treatment on her health in this way: "When I start to feel the angina pain trying to come on, I use my Relaxation Response to make the pain go away. To do this exercise, I usually unplug the phone so that I won't be distracted, and I sit in a straight-backed chair."

Sometimes, the angina sensation may strike while she is visiting friends or riding on public transportation. In these circumstances, she says, "I just close my eyes and go through my Relaxation Response exercise, and that feeling never develops into angina pain. Depending on the location I'm in, if I can't sit in a straight-backed chair, I simply breathe slowly and quietly and just say my two-word prayer, over and over on the out-breath. I can actually feel my heart rate become slower and slower, and there is a sense of calmness and peace. Again, the angina sensation never develops into a chest pain of any kind."

On a purely physical level, Roberta's experience has been a true success story. She says, "When I practice the Relaxation Response consistently, I stay absolutely free of angina pains for months and years at a time."

Just as important, the experience of eliciting the Relaxation Response through this meditative prayer has helped to reinforce and enhance Roberta's long-standing Christian faith. She says, "The fact that I'm very active, still alive, and can walk for ten to fifteen city blocks without exhaustion or angina, lets me know without a doubt that my faith in the Almighty has sustained me over all these years."

Healings of various types have historically had a tremendous personal and spiritual impact on those who have been given full health. Witness, for example, Jesus' healing of the blind man in the Gospel of John, chapter nine. There the one who was healed was ready to stand up boldly and defend his unpopular healer before the local authorities. Similarly, when Peter healed the lame man in Acts 3, the former cripple became something of an evangelist and preacher himself, as he walked about shouting the praises of God. Not only that, he was willing to stand beside Peter and John and defend them when they were brought up on charges before local governmental authorities.

In the case of Roberta, the improvement was not instantaneous, but its impact in bolstering and confirming her faith was significant. As Roberta perceived it, her improved health was related to the usual physiological effects of eliciting the Relaxation Response. At the same time, however, there was a spiritual dimension to this experience which had a beneficial, uplifting impact on her entire faith.

Often, I find that many deeply religious people are unaware that various forms of meditation are actually a part of their historic spiritual tradition. They may begin by using the Relaxation Response to treat their physical and psychological conditions. Beyond that, they may find they have learned a technique which they can use, as Roberta did, to enhance their spirituality.

Another of my patients, a woman named Edna, suffered from high blood pressure. We placed her on a program which involved eliciting the Relaxation Response through a prayer which was meaningful to her: "God have mercy on me." Then, after eliciting the Relaxation Response, she would frequently read spiritual literature and otherwise expose herself to beneficial influences which tended to reinforce her faith.

Before long, Edna discovered that her blood pressure had been significantly reduced. The effects of the meditative prayer that she was using began to reach far beyond her specific problem with hypertension. Among other things, she discovered that some problems she had suffered with insomnia began to be resolved. Various aches and pains she was experiencing also subsided.

Edna has also enjoyed significant spiritual benefits. She finds that with her prayer and meditation program—initially designed by us as a specific treatment for her high blood pressure—she now spends more time in communicating with her God. As a result, she is experiencing a greater sense of inner calmness and peace. She also tends to emphasize more the things she is thankful for in her life, rather than the things she has to worry about.

In both of these cases, the individuals moved naturally from Phase One of the Principle of the Maximum Mind—the elicitation of the Relaxation Response—into Phase Two. For them, Phase Two involved pursuing their normal religious activities: These included Bible-reading, studying spiritual literature and attending worship services and other religious meetings. Their minds were opened for further change as they moved into these various spiritual activities. As a result, as their health improved, their faith deepened and their spiritual understanding increased.

**2. Well-designed group religious experiences can make good use of the Principle of the Maximum Mind.** One such experience, which arose in the Roman Catholic church in Spain several decades ago, is called the *Cursillo*, or "a little course" in Christianity. This retreat-type experience, which also goes under the name of *Tres Dias* in the Presbyterian church and other Protestant traditions, has sometimes had a dramatic impact in changing the spirituality of those who attend. In many ways, this experience can provide a good illustration of the beneficial group application of the Principle of the Maximum Mind.

In one such *Cursillo*, which was conducted by a group of Episcopal churches in the Northeast, all those participating arrived on Thursday night and were expected to stay through Sunday afternoon. No one, except the team members conducting the religious exercises, knew exactly what to expect.

From the moment the participants arrived, they were exposed to what one person called "a religious boot-camp" experience. They attended one lecture after another, and heard inspirational explanations of the major principles of the Christian faith and the proper expressions of that faith in service and worship. Much additional time was set aside for contemplation, meditation and worship. These meetings were usually conducted in a chapel provided with candles and incense to enhance the sense of gravity.

During the weekend the participants were waited on constantly by the team members. They were literally "showered with love," as one person put it. Every day, they received a barrage of notes and gifts, which were known by the Spanish name *palanca*.

Soon, dramatic changes began to take place in a number of those who were participating. One woman said that for the first time, she learned what it meant to "fall in love with Jesus." Her experience before the *Cursillo* had certainly been characterized by commitment and deep faith. But a certain lilt and vitality had been lacking in her spirituality, and the changes which took place in her helped to fill that void.

Another woman underwent a kind of conversion. She had attended church regularly, but the experience had just been one part of her life, which she had pigeonholed for religious purposes. Now, she felt she had to allow the spirituality, which she had barely been experiencing before, to spill over into other aspects of her family and work life.

Still another participant, a man who had been consumed with many of the administrative aspects of his own churchmanship, realized as a result of the lectures and meditative experiences, that he should be spending more time with the needy. He resolved to participate regularly in a local program for the homeless.

An analysis of the *Cursillo* in terms of the Principle of the Maximum Mind reveals several interesting dynamics. One of my colleagues, who was able to attend a weekend of this type, put it this way: "First of all, we were opened up through the extensive and moving prayer times and worship experiences. Most people entered into a meditative state, which I'm sure in many cases involved the elicitation of the Relaxation Response. Sometimes, we sat in the darkened chapel and alternated between saying the liturgy, staring at the flickering candles and offering our own prayers and meditations.

"The most intense experiences of this type often took place in the evening, just before bedtime. After the service, every participant was instructed not to speak to anyone, but rather to go directly to their rooms and either read and meditate on the day's activities or go on to bed. Many people did spend some time reading and reflecting—and of course, that fits in directly with Phase Two of the Principle of the Maximum Mind. In other words, these people were opened up and then their minds were susceptible to further influence and change as a result of their reflection, reading and study.

"Also, the meditation experiences throughout the day were often followed by the lectures and other proclamations. To put this in more scientific terms, the meditative right-hemisphere activity of Phase One was followed by the word-oriented, analytical, left-hemisphere activity of Phase Two."

My friend is quick to point out, as I have so often done myself, that the complete spiritual impact of an experience like the *Cursillo* cannot be explained fully in biological or scientific categories. To be sure, the two hemispheres of the brain were probably actively at work during this experience. Perhaps it's best in this context to think of them as conduits for transcendent forces, rather than as explanations in themselves for the spiritual transformations that occurred.

This *Cursillo*-type experience, positive though it is, leads me to another, more negative and sometimes even dangerous spiritual side of the Principle of the Maximum Mind. I call this rather dark dimension the danger zone.

### *The Danger Zone*

Just as the Principle of the Maximum Mind can be used in a positive way to enhance a person's spiritual development, it can also be employed in what has been called a demonic fashion.

Take the approach used in a number of cults which have been publicized extensively over the past several decades. These groups have their initiates meditate or perform some repetitive activity, such as incessant chanting or simple, rhythmic dancing. In many cases, the new members are given little time to reflect or think about what is happening to them. Usually, those who are being inducted into the cult are accompanied by one of the guides or instructors, who bombard them with information and concepts designed to change their existing beliefs and commitment systems.

Those who are exposed to such an environment over a period of time begin to change. The repetitive activities and meditations open them up to change through the elicitation of the Relaxation Response. They are ushered into Phase One of the Principle of the Maximum Mind.

Then, through the cult's directors and a flood of specially selected information, their minds are altered into the patterns that cult leaders have chosen. In short, there really *is* a change which takes place in the physiological structure of the brains of those who have been exposed for long, intense periods to cultic indoctrination.

Many have wondered how such a large number of people could have been fooled into getting involved with the Jonestown cult, the commune founded by the Reverend Jim Jones in Guyana nearly ten years ago. As you'll recall, on November 18, 1978, U.S. Representative Leo Ryan and four other investigators were shot and killed at the Jonestown airstrip; and 911 followers of the Reverend Jones died by gunfire and also by drinking, at Jones's direction, cyanide-laced punch in the Jonestown jungle compound.

The followers of Jim Jones were not really fooled, at least not during the last, tragic phase of their experience at Jonestown. Rather, removed from other, more responsible mediating perspectives far away in the Guyana jungles, they apparently underwent a group transformation of their thinking processes as a result of an awful demonic application of the Principle of the Maximum Mind. Their spiritual commitments, their beliefs and their very thought patterns were so changed that they embarked on a path that ultimately led to their own self-destruction.

Much less extreme but still questionable applications of the Principle of the Maximum Mind have also found their way into the business world. Consider this report in the April 17, 1987, *New York Times*: "In their zeal to become more competitive, American employers have turned to motivational gurus who say they can change how employees think." The techniques used by the employers included meditation, relaxation, and visualizations, which are clearly applications of the Principle of the Maximum Mind.

I believe it's essential that these powerful techniques be controlled by the individual under the direction of his or her chosen maximum mind guide. Also, the individual should be comfortable with the philosophy of the program even *before* getting started on it.

Clearly we're dealing with a potent tool. Up to this point, I've emphasized the positive uses of the Principle of the Maximum Mind. I continue to believe that we should all understand and utilize the Principle, in the spiritual realm as well as in other parts of our lives. At the same time, we must always be aware of the possible dangers.

For this reason, I must emphasize how *absolutely essential* it is, especially when you start dealing with issues of ultimate reality and spirituality, to find a responsible guide to lead you during the inner transformations which you will surely experience. Cults are especially dangerous because they have not been tested over time and proven to be beneficial to their followers. For this reason that I am adamant about the importance of relying upon ancient faiths which have been proved to be safe and to promote altruistic teachings over centuries and even millennia.

Another concern, which is related to this cult problem, is the way a sense of mission can develop among those who have experienced exciting personal transformations. Your change of mind may be so profound and moving that you feel compelled to share it with your fellow human beings. There's nothing wrong with this attitude *per se*. In fact, there's a great deal that's right about it. Some of the greatest, most beneficial movements in human history have come from true believers who are totally committed to some cause or belief.

But there's also a danger here. It's natural, when you've had an intense inner transformation, to assume that you've found the only "true" way. Again, that belief, in itself, may not only be a positive thing but also an essential part of your inner drive and motivation emerging at last. It's the next step, however, which can begin to cause the problems. The intensity of your experience may blind you to the fact that others, from other traditions or belief systems, may also have undergone similar moving experiences that should be accorded the same respect you yourself expect. These people may be just as convinced as you are of the uniqueness of their particular insights.

So if you do develop a sense of mission as a result of your personal transformation, feel free to enjoy and revel in it. At the same time, try to put your experience in a community perspective. Above all, be tolerant and understanding of others who have also found ineffable, life-changing shifts of direction but have done so in a fashion different from yours.

Finally, just a word about modern-day television, radio and advertising: More often than we realize, our moral and spiritual values—and those of our family members—are influenced by what we see and hear on television and in various advertisements. The danger in this area escalates if you expose yourself to these media influences immediately after you've been opened up through the elicitation of the Relaxation Response.

Suppose you come in from a satisfying exercise session or you have just finished your prayers. You are then relatively more open to other influences. If you turned on the television, then you could be unduly influenced by the programming or advertising. In such a case, you risk undergoing undesirable changes in your thinking. After you finish your Relaxation Response session, you could choose to spend time enjoying your family, reading material that you believe to be beneficial, or otherwise focusing on positive, edifying subject matter.

Of course, it's ultimately up to you, as an independent, thinking individual, to select material from the belief system or personal philosophy which you feel is best suited for your own needs. But perhaps it's also wise to identify for yourself and consider the danger zones present in our culture before you make any final decisions. Understanding some of the pitfalls can be a useful first step in choosing the most beneficial spiritual path.

### *Developing a Spiritual Discipline*

As you move to develop your own spirituality, here are the two phases of the Principle of the Maximum Mind which can open you up to beneficial transformations. Remember, the Principle has no power in itself to teach you about the ultimate truth or the nature of God. It's only a human capacity that can help to open you up to circumstances which can enhance your own spirituality.

### *Phase One*

**Step 1:** Pick a focus word or short phrase that's firmly rooted in your personal belief system. As we've already seen, a Christian person might choose the opening words of Psalm 23, "The Lord is my shepherd"; a Jewish person, "Shalom"; a nonreligious individual, a neutral word like "one" or "peace."

**Step 2:** Sit quietly in a comfortable position.

**Step 3:** Close your eyes.

**Step 4:** Relax your muscles.

**Step 5:** Breathe slowly and naturally and, as you do, repeat your focus word or phrase as you exhale.

**Step 6:** Assume a passive attitude. Don't worry about how well you're doing. When other thoughts come to mind, simply say to yourself, "Oh, well," and gently return to the repetition.

**Step 7:** Continue for ten to twenty minutes.

**Step 8:** Practice the technique once or twice daily.

### *Phase Two*

Most likely, you already know the particular spiritual tradition that interests you or seems to hold the most promise for your inner development. Rather than attempt to act as a kind of "one-minute theologian," I would urge you to review the basic texts of your faith and expose yourself to those words and teachings. It's especially important in spiritual transformations to find a competent spiritual director, such as a priest, minister or rabbi, in whom you have trust and who agrees with your goals.

With these as with any spiritual considerations, you're dealing with perhaps the most important issues you'll ever face, such as your basic moral values and your world view. Please treat this area of change with appropriate sensitivity.

# 9.

## *Mountaintops of the Mind*

As research into the Principle of the Maximum Mind continues, what predictions can we make for the future?

I see several major frontiers awaiting further exploration. These include the self-controlled "marshaling" of brain chemicals and an expansion of the understanding and use of the placebo effect, and a broader use of the Principle of the Maximum Mind as an aid to spiritual, intellectual and athletic development. Now, let's take a closer look at each of these three areas.

### *The "Marshaling" of Brain Chemicals and the Placebo Effect*

In earlier chapters of this book, I've discussed how the cells of the brain communicate or connect with each other through chemicals called neurotransmitters. Where brain connections are used over and over again, they become established pathways or wirings. These connections hold our memories; in fact, they *are* our memories.

Thus, your brain-cell connections can remember a headache and can also remember feelings of well-being. Furthermore, they can remember the relief brought about naturally or by the taking of a medication—and this particular capacity offers great potential for medical treatment.

I believe that, through the use of the Principle of the Maximum Mind, it will be possible to tap into pathways that remember the relief of a headache or other pain. Then, the Principle could be utilized to bring about relief through action of the *same* neurotransmitters that were active in stopping the pain when, for example, you took medication.

All this is not as outrageous as it might sound at first. Researchers have discovered that some of the drugs we take for pain relief act as well as they do because they mimic neurotransmitters which we already have in our brains. These mimicked neurotransmitters, which scientists group under the term "ligands," serve as a kind of key which unlocks certain responses in the brain. Both the drugs *and* the neurotransmitters are capable of serving as keys in this respect.

For example, the drug morphine relieves pain and

produces a sense of euphoria—and so do the morphine-like neurotransmitters, the endorphins. Recently, we've learned that jogging and other natural activities can release endorphins and produce a morphinelike effect, all without drugs.

Undoubtedly, there are many other neurotransmitters which can also produce the same or similar effects as drugs—if we can just learn how to release them in a more controlled way. It's been proposed, for example, that the so-called mood-tranquilizing drugs, like Valium and Librium, are effective because they mimic neurotransmitters which we already possess. Perhaps we can learn how more effectively to "turn on" neurotransmitters through appropriate thought patterns.

How could we achieve such a result? I believe that through the use of the Principle of the Maximum Mind, we should be able to train ourselves to call forth these internal chemicals. Thus we may very well have the inner potential for pain relief and other enhancements of our well-being without the use of drugs.

Further research should also give us a better understanding of the placebo effect, and also suggest practical uses for this phenomenon. For one thing, we should increase our knowledge of the physiological basis of the healings performed by those who practice laying on of hands. Is there, as some claim, the transmission of energies, powers, or forces from the healer to the patient? Or are healings related more to the patient's *belief* in the healer's capacities to cure? Do we in effect remember what it was to be well and then re-create "wellness" connections in our brains? In a similar fashion, do inactive substances such as sugar pills bring about their healthful placebo effects because we believe them to be active, effective medications? Can these substances marshal "remembered wellness"? The answer to these questions and others like them await further research.

Of course, there are many worthwhile drugs that we don't possess within ourselves as neurotransmitters. Consequently, their use as medications will continue to be necessary. Penicillin and tetracycline are two such agents. In addition, we obviously won't be able to replace the great healing capabilities of modern surgery through a marshaling of brain chemicals.

You'll recall that about 75 percent of the illnesses that bring the average patient to the doctor are considered to be in the realm of mind-body interactions. Clearly, a proper application of the Principle of the Maximum Mind could play a major role in this very large aspect of medical practice. To put this another way, an understanding and application of the Principle could help us treat those ailments which fall between what modern medicine and surgery can handle on the one hand, and what psychiatry has to offer on the other.

Application of the Principle of the Maximum Mind would also lead to a more personalized, less technological and less expensive practice of medicine. In the first place, to improve health, we would make more use of our own personal thought patterns and be less dependent on impersonal medications and devices. Second, use of the Principle would necessitate that a physician or other health-care provider become a maximum mind guide. As a result, the physician would need a more intimate knowledge of each patient's deep-seated needs and beliefs. Finally, a less expensive practice of medicine could evolve because utilization of the Principle is probably the most efficient pathway into all forms of effective self-help.

### *Fitness, the Intellect and the Spiritual Side*

I can also foresee a much wider application of the Principle of the Maximum Mind in athletic, educational and religious instruction. This movement is already occurring at many schools and athletic training facilities.

On the spiritual side, it will be important for religious leaders and organizations to distinguish between what is a *human capacity*, available to people of all faiths, and what is the *inviolable substance* of their belief, unique to their own tradition toward which our human capacity gropes for understanding. Those who perceive that the Principle of the Maximum Mind focuses on a human capacity, not on spiritual substance, will increasingly utilize the Principle to enhance spiritual discipline.

• • •

As we near the end of this exploration of the potential of our maximum minds, on one level I hope what I've been saying has made sense; I hope that the left hemisphere of your brain has grasped these points, even though many of them are firmly rooted in that nonverbal right hemisphere. Perhaps in the process, you've already managed to change a few of the resistant, negative inferences that may have constrained the productive operation of your left hemisphere.

As a final exercise, let me suggest that you end with a practical application of the Principle of the Maximum Mind. To get some of these concepts and techniques firmly in mind so that you can use them to change your own life in the future, you might first speak to a maximum mind guide. Then, you could try entering into Phase One by eliciting the Relaxation Response.

Next, go into Phase Two by glancing back over the book and rereading sections that are of particular interest to you. As you look back, ponder the messages that you've received and decide what changes you need to make in your own life in the immediate future. It's my fervent hope that this book will not simply serve as a pleasant reading break in your life, but will also act as an open door, offering a way to your desired important personal transformations.

Using the Principle of the Maximum Mind, so simple to learn and practice, you too can—and will—enjoy the benefits of more positive, "whole brain" existence. You can tap the awesome capabilities of your own, unique Maximum Mind.

What happens next will be up to you. You have a choice. It's your Maximum Mind, to use with all its marvelous capacities.

# *Bibliography*

*Chapter* **1.**

Badawi, K., et al. "Electrophysiologic Characteristics of Respiratory Suspension Periods Occurring During the Practice of the Transcendental Meditation Program." *Psychosomatic Medicine* 46 (1984): 267–276.
Beary, J. F., and Benson, H. "A Simple Psychophysiologic Technique Which Elicits the Relaxation Response." *Psychosomatic Medicine* 36 (1974): 115–120.
Benson, H. *Beyond the Relaxation Response*. New York: Times Books, 1984.
———. *The Mind/Body Effect*. New York: Simon and Schuster, 1979.
———. *The Relaxation Response*. New York: William Morrow, 1975.

———. "The Relaxation Response and the Treatment of Anxiety." In *Psychiatric Update. The American Psychiatric Association Annual Review. Volume III*, edited by L. Grinspoon. Washington, D.C.: American Psychiatric Press, 1984.

———. "Systemic Hypertension and the Relaxation Response." *New England Journal of Medicine* 296 (1977): 1152–1156.

———. "Your Innate Asset for Combatting Stress." *Harvard Business Review* 52 (1974): 49–60.

Benson, H.; Alexander, S.; and Feldman, C. L. "Decreased Premature Ventricular Contractions Through the Use of the Relaxation Response in Patients with Stable Ischemic Heart Disease." *Lancet* ii (1975): 380–382.

Benson, H.; Arns, P. A.; and Hoffman, J. W. "The Relaxation Response and Hypnosis." *International Journal of Clinical and Experimental Hypnosis* 29 (1981): 259–270.

Benson, H.; Beary, J. F.; and Carol, M. P. "The Relaxation Response." *Psychiatry* 37 (1974): 37–46.

Benson, H.; Klemchuk, H. P.; and Graham, J. R. "The Usefulness of the Relaxation Response in the Therapy of Headache." *Headache* 14 (1974): 49–52.

Benson, H.; Pomeranz, B.; and Kutz, I. "Pain and the Relaxation Response." In *Textbook of Pain*, edited by P. D. Wall and R. Melzack. London: Churchill Livingstone, 1984.

Benson, H., et al. "Continuous Measurement of Oxygen Consumption and Carbon Dioxide Elimination During a Wakeful Hypometabolic State." *Journal of Human Stress* 1 (1975): 37–44.

Benson, H., et al. "Decreased Blood Pressure in Borderline Hypertensive Patients Who Practiced Meditation." *Journal of Chronic Disease* 27 (1974): 163–169.

Benson, H., et al. "Decreased Blood Pressure in Pharmacologically Treated Hypertensive Patients Who Regularly Elicited the Relaxation Response." *Lancet* i (1974): 289–291.

Benson, H., et al. "Treatment of Anxiety: A Comparison of the Usefulness of Self-Hypnosis and a Meditational Relaxation Technique." *Psychotherapy and Psychosomatics* 30 (1978): 229–242.

Carrington, P., et al. "The Use of Meditation-Relaxation Techniques for the Management of Stress in a Working Population." *Journal of Occupational Medicine* 22 (1980): 221–231.

Farrow, J. T., and Hebert, J. "Breath Suspension During Transcendental Meditation Technique." *Psychosomatic Medicine* 44 (1982): 133–153.

Fentress, D. W., et al. "Biofeedback and Relaxation-Response Training in the Treatment of Pediatric Migraine." *Developmental Medicine and Child Neurology* 28 (1986): 139–146.

Gazzaniga, M. S. *The Social Brain*. New York: Basic Books, 1985.

Gazzaniga, M. S., and LeDoux, J. *The Integrated Mind*. New York: Plenum, 1978.

Greenwood, M. M., and Benson, H. "The Efficacy of Progressive Relaxation in Systematic Desensitization and a Proposal for an Alternative Competitive Response—the Relaxation Response." *Behavior Research Therapy* 15 (1977): 337–343.

Gyatso Tenzin. "Compassion in Global Politics." *Tibet News Review* 6 (1986): 12–19.

Hoffman, J. W., et al. "Reduced Sympathetic Nervous System Responsivity Associated with the Relaxation Response." *Science* 215 (1982): 190–192.

Kutz, I.; Borysenko, J. Z.; and Benson, H. "Meditation and Psychotherapy: A Rationale for the Integration of Dynamic Psychotherapy, the Relaxation Response and Mindfulness Meditation." *American Journal of Psychiatry* 142 (1985): 1–8.

Lehmann, J. W.; Goodale, I. L.; and Benson, H. "Reduced Pupillary Sensitivity to Topical Phenylephrine Associated with the Relaxation Response." *Journal of Human Stress* 12 (1986): 101–104.

Orme-Johnson, D. W., and Haynes, C. T. "EEG Phase Coherence, Pure Consciousness, Creativity, and TM-Sidhi Experiences." *Neuroscience* 13 (1981): 211–217.

Peters, R. K.; Benson, H.; and Peters, J. M. "Daily Relaxation Response Breaks in a Working Population: 2. Blood Pressure." *American Journal of Public Health* 67 (1977): 954–959.

Peters, R. K.; Benson, H.; and Porter, D. "Daily Relaxation Response Breaks in a Working Population: 1. Health, Performance and Well-Being." *American Journal of Public Health* 67 (1977): 946–953.

Sperry, R. W. "Brain Bisection and Mechanisms of Consciousness." In *Brain and Conscious Experience*, edited by J. C. Eccles. New York: Springer, 1966.

———. "Cerebral Organization and Behavior." *Science* 133 (1961): 1749–1757.

Wallace, R. K., and Benson, H. "The Physiology of Meditation." *Scientific American* 226 (1972): 84–90.

Wallace, R. K.; Benson, H.; and Wilson, A. F. "A Wakeful Hypometabolic State." *American Journal of Physiology* 221 (1971): 795–799

Warrenburg, S., and Pagano, R. "Meditation and Hemispheric Specialization I: Absorbed Attention in Long-Term Adherence." *Imagination, Cognition and Personality* 2 (1982–83): 211–229.

## *Chapter* 2.

Benson, H. *Beyond the Relaxation Response*. New York: Times Books, 1984.

———. "Body Temperature Changes During the Practice of gTum-mo Yoga." *Nature* 298 (1982): 402.

———. *The Relaxation Response*. New York: William Morrow, 1975.

Benson, H., et al. "Body Temperature Changes During the Practice of gTum-mo Yoga." *Nature* 295 (1982): 234–236.

Black, I., as cited in "Nerve Activity Alters Neurotransmitter Synthesis." *Science* 232 (1986): 1500–1501.

David-Neel, A. *Magic and Mystery in Tibet*. New York: Penguin Books, 1971.

Gazzaniga, M. S. *The Social Brain*. New York: Basic Books, 1985.

Gazzaniga, M. S., and LeDoux, J. *The Integrated Mind*. New York: Plenum, 1978.

Goddard, G. V., and Douglas, R. M. "Does the Engram of Kindling Model the Engram of Long-Term Memory?" In *Kindling*, edited by J. A. Wada and R. T. Ross. New York: Raven Press, 1976.

Hoffman, J. W., et al. "Reduced Sympathetic Nervous

System Responsivity Associated with the Relaxation Response." *Science* 215 (1982): 190–192.

Kutz, I.; Borysenko, J. Z.; and Benson, H. "Meditation and Psychotherapy: A Rationale for the Integration of Dynamic Psychotherapy, the Relaxation Response and Mindfulness Meditation." *American Journal of Psychiatry* 142 (1985): 1–8.

LeDoux, J. E.; Wilson, D. H.; Gazzaniga, M. S. "A Divided Mind: Observations on the Conscious Properties of the Separated Hemispheres." *Annals of Neurology* 2 (1977): 417–421.

Myers, R. E., and Sperry, R. W. "Interocular Transfer of a Visual Form Discrimination Habit in Cats After Section of the Optic Chiasm and Corpus Callosum." *Anatomical Record* 115 (1953): 351–352.

Nauta, W. J. H., and Feirtag, M. *Fundamental Neuroanatomy*. New York: W. H. Freeman, 1986.

Pert, C. B., et al. "Neuropeptides and Their Receptors: A Psychosomatic Network." *Journal of Immunology* 135 (1985): 8205–8265.

Racine, R.; Tuff, L.; and Zaide, J. "Kindling, Unit Discharge Patterns, and Neural Plasticity." In *Kindling*, edited by J. A. Wada and R. T. Ross. New York: Raven Press, 1976.

Sperry, R. W. "Brain Bisection and Mechanisms of Consciousness." In *Brain and Conscious Experience*, edited by J. C. Eccles. New York: Springer, 1966.

———. "Cerebral Organization and Behavior." *Science* 133 (1961): 1749–1757.

———. "Lateral Specialization of the Cerebral Function in the Surgically Separated Hemispheres." In *The Psychophysiology of Thinking*, edited by F. J. Mc-

Guigan and R. A. Schoonover. New York: Academic Press, 1973.

Squire, L. R. "Mechanisms of Memory." *Science* 232 (1986): 1612–1619.

## Chapter 3.

Badawi, K., et al. "Electrophysiologic Characteristics of Respiratory Suspension Periods Occurring During the Practice of the Transcendental Meditation Program." *Psychosomatic Medicine* 46 (1984): 267–276.

Benson, H. *Beyond the Relaxation Response*. New York: Times Books, 1984.

———. *The Mind/Body Effect*. New York: Simon and Schuster, 1979.

Benson, H.; Arns, P. A.; and Hoffman, J. W. "The Relaxation Response and Hypnosis." *International Journal of Clinical and Experimental Hypnosis* 29 (1981): 259–270.

Benson, H., and Epstein, M. D. "The Placebo Effect. A Neglected Asset in the Care of Patients." *Journal of the American Medical Association* 232 (1975): 1225–1227.

Benson, H., and McCallie, D. P., Jr. "Angina Pectoris and the Placebo Effect." *New England Journal of Medicine* 300 (1979): 1424–1429.

*Brain and Conscious Experience,* edited by J. C. Eccles. New York: Springer, 1966.

Cannon, W. B. " 'Voodoo' Death." *American Anthropologist* 44 (1942): 169–181.

Cebelin, M., and Hirsch, C. S. "Human Stress Cardiomyopathy." *Human Pathology* 11 (1980): 123–132

Dean, S. R. "Metapsychiatry: The Confluence of Psychiatry and Mysticism." In *Psychiatry and Mysticism*, edited by S. R. Dean. Chicago: Nelson-Hall, 1975.

Egbert, L. D., et al. "Reduction of Postoperative Pain by Encouragement and Instruction of Patients." *New England Journal of Medicine* 270 (1964): 825–827.

Eliot, T. S. *Four Quartets*. New York: New Directions, 1970.

Engel, G. L. A. "Sudden and Rapid Death During Psychological Stress." *Annals of Internal Medicine* 74 (1971): 771–782.

Farrow, J. T., and Hebert, J. "Breath Suspension During Transcendental Meditation Technique." *Psychosomatic Medicine* 44 (1982): 133–153.

Festinger, L. *A Theory of Cognitive Dissonance*. Stanford, California: Stanford University Press, 1957.

Fifkova, E., and VanHarreveld, A. "Long-Lasting Morphological Changes in Dendritic Spines of Dentate Granule Cells Following Stimulation of the Entorhinal Area." *Journal of Neurocytology* 6 (1977): 211–230.

Gazzaniga, M. S. *The Social Brain*. New York: Basic Books, 1985.

Gliedman, J. "Scientists in Search of a Soul." *Science Digest* 89 (1982): 77–79, 105.

Goddard, G. V., and Douglas, R. M. "Does the Engram of Kindling Model the Engram of Long-Term Memory?" In *Kindling*, edited by J. A. Wada and R. T. Ross. New York: Raven Press, 1976.

Goodwin, D. W. *Anxiety*. New York: Oxford University Press, 1986.

Joy, R. M. "The Effects of Neurotoxicants on Kindling and Kindled Seizures." *Fundamental and Applied Toxicology* 5 (1985): 41–65.

Kutz, I.; Borysenko, J. Z.; and Benson, H. "Meditation and Psychotherapy: A Rationale for the Integration of Dynamic Psychotherapy, the Relaxation Response and Mindfulness Meditation." *American Journal of Psychiatry* 142 (1985): 1–8.

Lee, K. S., et al. "Brief Bursts of High-Frequency Stimulation Produce Two Types of Structural Change in the Rat Hippocampus." *Journal of Neurophysiology* 44 (1980): 247–258.

Mills, J. "Changes in Moral Attitudes Following Temptation." *Journal of Personality* 26 (1958): 517–521.

Milton, G. W. "Self-Willed Death or the Bone-Pointing Syndrome." *Lancet* i (1973): 1435–1436.

Orme-Johnson, D. W., and Haynes, C. T. "EEG Phase Coherence, Pure Consciousness, Creativity, and TM-Sidhi Experiences." *Neuroscience* 13 (1981): 211–217.

Penfield, W. "Interview." *Maclean's Magazine*, April 19, 1976.

———. *The Mystery of the Mind*. Princeton, New Jersey: Princeton University Press, 1975.

Racine, R.; Tuff, L.; and Zaide, J. "Kindling, Unit Discharge Patterns and Neural Plasticity." In *Kindling*, edited by J. A. Wada and R. T. Ross. New York: Raven Press, 1976.

Sperry, R. W. "Mind, Brain and Humanist Values." In *New Views of the Nature of Man*. Chicago: University of Chicago Press, 1965.

———. *Science and Moral Priority: Merging Mind, Brain*

*and Human Values*. New York: Columbia University Press, 1983.
Warrenburg, S., and Pagano, R. "Meditation and Hemispheric Specialization I: Absorbed Attention in Long-Term Adherence." *Imagination, Cognition and Personality* 2 (1982–83): 211–229.
Wolf, S. "Effects of Suggestion and Conditioning on the Action of Chemical Agents in Human Subjects." *Journal of Clinical Investigation* 29 (1950): 100–109.
Wolf, S., and Dinsky, R. H. "Effects of Placebo Administration and Occurrence of Toxic Reactions." *Journal of the American Medical Association* 155 (1954): 339–341.

*Chapter* **4.**

Asaf, G. (Powell, G. H.). As cited in *Bartlett's Familiar Quotations*. Boston: Little, Brown, 1980.
Benson, H. *Beyond the Relaxation Response*. New York: Times Books, 1984.
———. *The Relaxation Response*. New York: William Morrow, 1975.
Coué, É. *Self-Mastery Through Conscious Autosuggestion*. New York: 1922.
Epictitus. *The Discourses as Reported by Arrian*. Translated by W. A. Oldfather. Cambridge, Massachusetts: Harvard University Press, 1946.
Franklin, B. *Benjamin Franklin: An Autobiographical Portrait*. New York: Macmillan, 1969.
———. *Poor Richard's Almanac*. Philadelphia, Pennsylvania: Saunders, 1732.

Hale, E. E., Jr. *The Life and Letters of Edward Everett Hale.* Boston: Little, Brown, 1917.

Kutz, I.; Borysenko, J. Z.; and Benson, H. "Meditation and Psychotherapy: A Rationale for the Integration of Dynamic Psychotherapy, the Relaxation Response and Mindfulness Meditation." *American Journal of Psychiatry* 142 (1985): 1–8.

Lubbock, J. *The Pleasures of Life.* London: Macmillan and Company, 1887.

Peale, N. V. *The Power of Positive Thinking.* Greenwich, Connecticut: Fawcett Crest, 1956.

Prior, M. "Epistle to Fleetwood Shepherd," as cited in *The Home Book of Quotations: Classical and Modern.* New York: Dodd, Mead, 1964.

Publilius Syrus. *The Moral Sayings of Publilius Syrus.* Translated by D. Lyman. Cleveland, Ohio: L. E. Barnard and Company, 1856.

Schuller, R. H. *It's Possible.* Old Tappan, New Jersey: Fleming H. Revell, 1978.

———. *Be Happy You Are Loved.* Nashville: Thomas Nelson, 1986.

Wordsworth, W. *The Complete Poetical Works of Wordsworth.* Boston: Houghton Mifflin, 1932.

## *Chapter* 5.

Benson, H. *Beyond the Relaxation Response.* New York: Times Books, 1984.

———. *The Mind/Body Effect.* New York: Simon and Schuster, 1979.

———. *The Relaxation Response.* New York: William Morrow, 1975.

———. "The Relaxation Response and the Treatment of Anxiety." In *Psychiatric Update. The American Psychiatric Association Annual Review. Volume III*, edited by L. Grinspoon. Washington, D.C.: American Psychiatric Press, 1984.

———. "Systemic Hypertension and the Relaxation Response." *New England Journal of Medicine* 296 (1977): 1152–1156.

Benson, H., and McCallie, D. P., Jr. "Angina Pectoris and the Placebo Effect." *New England Journal of Medicine* 300 (1979): 1424–1429.

Benson, H.; Alexander, S.; and Feldman, C. L. "Decreased Premature Ventricular Contractions Through the Use of the Relaxation Response in Patients with Stable Ischemic Heart Disease." *Lancet* ii (1975): 380–382.

Benson, H.; Arns, P. A.; and Hoffman, J. W. "The Relaxation Response and Hypnosis." *International Journal of Clinical and Experimental Hypnosis* 29 (1981): 259–270.

Benson, H.; Klemchuk, H. P.; and Graham, J. R. "The Usefulness of the Relaxation Response in the Therapy of Headache." *Headache* 14 (1974): 49–52.

Benson, H.; Pomeranz, B.; and Kutz, I. "Pain and the Relaxation Response." In *Textbook of Pain*, edited by P. D. Wall and R. Melzack. London: Churchill Livingstone, 1984.

Benson, H., et al. "Decreased Blood Pressure in Borderline Hypertensive Subjects Who Practiced Meditation." *Journal of Chronic Disease* 27 (1974): 163–169.

Benson, H., et al. "Decreased Blood Pressure in Pharmacologically Treated Hypertensive Patients Who

Regularly Elicited the Relaxation Response." *Lancet* i (1974): 289–291.

Benson, H., et al. "Treatment of Anxiety: A Comparison of the Usefulness of Self-Hypnosis and a Meditational Relaxation Technique." *Psychotherapy and Psychosomatics* 30 (1978): 229–242.

Black, I. B., et al. "Biochemistry of Information Storage in the Nervous System." *Science* 236 (1987): 1263–1268.

Carrington, P., et al. "The Use of Meditation-Relaxation Techniques for the Management of Stress in a Working Population." *Journal of Occupational Medicine* 22 (1980): 221–231.

Cousins, N. *The Healing Heart*. New York: W. W. Norton, 1983.

Deadwyler, S. A., et al. "Long-Lasting Changes in the Spontaneous Activity of Hippocampal Neurons Following Stimulation of the Entorhinal Cortex." *Brain Research Bulletin* 18 (1976): 1–7.

Delanoy, R. L.; Tucci, D. L.; and Gold, R. E. "Amphetamine Effects on Long-Term Potential in Dentate Granule Cells." *Pharmacology, Biochemistry and Behavior* 18 (1983): 137–139.

*The Dhammapada, Sayings of the Buddha*. Translated by T. Byram. New York: Vintage Books, 1976.

Dunne, F. P., as cited in *The Home Book of Quotations: Classical and Modern*. New York: Dodd, Mead, 1964.

Emerson, R. W. *Essays and Lectures/ Ralph Waldo Emerson*. New York: The Library of America, 1983.

Everly, G. S. "Biological Foundations of Psychiatric Sequelae in Trauma and Stress-Related Disorders of Arousal." Paper presented at the Eighth National Trauma Symposium, University of Maryland School of Medicine, Baltimore, Maryland, November, 1985.

Fentress, D. W., et al. "Biofeedback and Relaxation-Response Training in the Treatment of Pediatric Migraine." *Developmental Medicine and Child Neurology* 28 (1986): 139–146.

Fifkova, E., and VanHarreveld, A. "Long-Lasting Morphological Changes in Dendritic Spines of Dentate Granule Cells Following Stimulation of the Entorhinal Area." *Journal of Neurocytology* 6 (1977): 211–230.

Fry, J. *Profiles of Disease: A Study in the Natural History of Common Disease*. Edinburgh: E. and S. Livingstone, 1966.

Galin, D. "Implications for Psychiatry of Left and Right Cerebral Specialization." *Archives of General Psychiatry* 31 (1974): 572–583.

Goddard, G. V., and Douglas, R. M. "Does the Engram of Kindling Model the Engram of Long-Term Memory?" In *Kindling*, edited by J. A. Wada and R. T. Ross. New York: Raven Press, 1976.

Goleman, D. "Buddhist and Western Psychology: Some Commonalities and Differences." *Journal of Transpersonal Psychology* 13 (1981): 125–136.

———. "Meditation and Consciousness: An Asian Approach to Mental Health." *American Journal of Psychotherapy* 30 (1977): 41–54.

Goodwin, D. W. *Anxiety*. New York: Oxford University Press, 1986.

Govinda, L. A. *Creative Meditation and Multi-Dimensional Consciousness*. Wheaton, Illinois: Theosophical Publishing House, 1978.

Greenwood, M. M., and Benson, H. "The Efficacy of Progressive Relaxation in Systematic Desensitization and a Proposal for an Alternative Competitive Response—The Relaxation Response." *Behavior Research Therapy* 15 (1977): 337–343.

Hoffman, J. W., et al. "Reduced Sympathetic Nervous System Responsivity Associated with the Relaxation Response." *Science* 215 (1982): 190–192.

Ingelfinger, F. J. "Medicine: Meritorious or Meretricious." *Science* 200 (1978): 942–946.

Joy, R. M. "The Effects of Neurotoxicants on Kindling and Kindled Seizures." *Fundamental and Applied Toxicology* 5 (1985): 41–65.

Kabat-Zinn, J. "An Outpatient Program in Behavioral Medicine for Chronic Pain Based on the Practice of Mindfulness Meditation: Theoretical Considerations and Preliminary Results." *General Hospital Psychiatry* 4 (1982): 33–48.

Kabat-Zinn, J.; Lipworth, L.; and Burney, R. "The Clinical Use of Mindfulness Meditation for the Self-Regulation of Chronic Pain." *Journal of Behavioral Medicine* 8 (1985): 163–190.

Keats, J. *The Poetical Works of John Keats*. Edited by H. Buxton Forman. London: Oxford University Press, 1937.

Kiecolt-Glaser, J. K., and Glaser, R. "Psychological Influences on Immunity." *Psychosomatics* 9 (1986): 621–624.

Kiecolt-Glaser, J. K., et al. "Marital Quality, Marital Disruption and Immune Function." *Psychosomatic Medicine* 49 (1987): 13–34.

Kiecolt-Glaser, J. K., et al. "Modulation of Cellular Immunity in Medical Students." *Journal of Behavioral Medicine* 9 (1986): 5–21.

Kiecolt-Glaser, J. K., et al. "Psychosocial Enhancement

of the Immunocompetence in a Geriatric Population." *Health Psychology* 4 (1985): 25–41.

Kutz, I.; Borysenko, J. Z.; and Benson, H. "Meditation and Psychotherapy: A Rationale for the Integration of Dynamic Psychotherapy, the Relaxation Response and Mindfulness Meditation." *American Journal of Psychiatry* 142 (1985): 1–8.

Laparello, T., et al. "Influences of Suggestion on Airway Reactivity in Asthmatic Subjects." *Psychosomatic Medicine* 30 (1968): 819–825.

Lee, K. S., et al. "Brief Bursts of High-Frequency Stimulation Produce Two Types of Structural Change in the Rat Hippocampus." *Journal of Neurophysiology* 44 (1980): 247–258.

McFadden, E. R., Jr., et al. "The Mechanism of Action of Suggestion in the Induction of Acute Asthma Attacks." *Psychosomatic Medicine* 31 (1969): 134–143.

Monroe, R. "Limbic Ictus and Typical Psychosis." *Journal of Nervous and Mental Disease* 170 (1982): 711–716.

Narada, M. *A Manual of Abhidhamma*. Kandiy, Ceylon: Buddhist Publication Society, 1968.

Noy, P. "Insight and Creativity." *Journal of the American Psychoanalytical Association* 26 (1978): 717–748.

Nyanaponika, M. *The Heart of Buddhist Meditation*. London: Rider, 1962.

Nyrén, O., et al. "Absence of Therapeutic Benefit from Antacids or Cimetidine in Non-Ulcer Dyspepsia." *New England Journal of Medicine* 314 (1986): 339–343.

Peters, R. K.; Benson, H.; and Peters, J. M. "Daily Relaxation Response Breaks in a Working Population: 2. Blood Pressure." *American Journal of Public Health* 67 (1977): 954–959.

Peters, R. K.; Benson, H.; and Porter, D. "Daily Relaxation Response Breaks in a Working Population: 1. Health, Performance and Well-Being." *American Journal of Public Health* 67 (1977): 946–953.

Racine, R.; Tuff, L.; and Zaide, J. "Kindling, Unit Discharge Patterns and Neural Plasticity." In *Kindling*, edited by J. A. Wada and R. T. Ross. New York: Raven Press, 1976.

Richter, J. As cited in *Science 86* 7 (1986): 6.

Sanford, A. M. *The Healing Light*. Plainfield, New Jersey, Logos International, 1972.

Shakespeare, W. *The Complete Works of William Shakespeare*. New York: W. J. Black, 1937.

Wielgosz, A. T., and Earp, J. A. "Perceived Vulnerability to Serious Heart Disease and Persistent Pain in Patients with Minimal or No Coronary Disease." *Psychosomatic Medicine* 48 (1986): 118–124.

*Chapter* **6.**

Benson, H. *The Relaxation Response*. New York: William Morrow, 1975.

Blatt, H. "Positive Thinking Helps." *New York Daily News*. October 27, 1986.

Borges, R. "Healthy Dose of Optimism." *The Boston Globe*. September 10, 1986.

Cash, T. F.; Winstead, B. A.; and Janda, L. H. "The Great American Shape-Up." *Psychology Today* 20 (1986): 30–37.

Cooper, K. H. *The Aerobics Program for Total Well Being*. New York: Bantam Books, 1983.

Editors of Sports Illustrated. *Sports Illustrated Squash.* New York: J. B. Lippincott, 1971.

Faulkner, W. *Essays, Speeches and Public Letters*. Edited by J. B. Meriwether. New York: Random House, 1966.

Fixx, J. F. *The Complete Book of Running*. New York: Random House, 1977.

Homer. *The Iliad*. Translated by R. Fitzgerald. Garden City, New York: Anchor Press, Doubleday, 1974.

Johnson, R. S. "Lloyd Advances to Open Semifinal." *New York Times*. September 4, 1986.

Kiphuth, R. J. H. *Swimming*. New York: A. S. Barnes, 1942.

Kosslyn, S. M., et al. "Individual Differences in Mental Imagery: A Computational Analysis." *Cognition* 18 (1984): 195–243.

Kostrubala, T. *The Joy of Running*. New York: Lippincott, 1976.

Lown, B. "Verbal Conditioning of Angina Pectoris During Exercise Testing." *American Journal of Cardiology* 40 (1977): 630–634.

Nicholi, A. M., Jr. "Psychiatric Consultation in Professional Football." *New England Journal of Medicine* 316 (1987): 1095–1100.

Noble, H. B. " 'Zone' Is Winning Territory." *New York Times*. September 5, 1986.

*Royal Canadian Air Force Exercise Plans for Physical Fitness.* New York: Pocket Books, 1962.

Ruskin, J. *The Genius of John Ruskin*. Edited by J. S. Rosenberg. New York: G. Braziller, 1963.

Service, R. W. *Collected Poems*. New York: Dodd, Mead, 1972.

Shakespeare, W. *The Complete Works of William Shakespeare*. New York: W. J. Black, 1937.
Tennyson, A. *The Poetical Works of Tennyson*. Edited by G. R. Strange. Boston: Houghton Mifflin, 1974.
Thackeray, W. M. *The Virginians*. New York: Dutton, 1965.
Warshal, D. "Effects of T. M. Technique on Normal and Jendrassik Reflex Time." *Perceptual and Motor Skills* 50 (1980): 1103–1106.

## *Chapter* 7.

Abrams, A. I. "The Effects of Meditation on Elementary School Students." *Dissertation Abstracts International* 37 (9-A) (1977): 5689.
Benson, H. *The Relaxation Response*. New York: William Morrow, 1975.
Bridges, R. S. *The Testament of Beauty; A Poem in Four Books*. New York: Oxford University Press, 1930.
Browning, R. *The Complete Poetical Works of Browning*. Boston: Houghton Mifflin, 1895.
Churchill, C., as cited in *The Home Book of Quotations: Classical and Modern*. New York: Dodd, Mead, 1964.
Einstein, A. *Einstein, A., 1879–1955—Addresses, Essays, Lectures*, edited by M. Goldsmith, A. Mackay and J. Woudhysen. New York: Pergamon Press, 1980.
Emerson, R. W. *Essays and Lectures/Ralph Waldo Emerson*. New York: The Library of America, 1983.
Fiebert, M. S., and Mead, T. M. "Meditation and Ac-

ademic Performance." *Perceptual and Motor Skills* 53 (1981): 447–450.

Gardner, H. *Art, Mind and Brain: A Cognitive Approach to Creativity*. New York: Basic Books, 1982.

———. *Frames of Mind: The Theory of Multiple Intelligences*. New York: Basic Books, 1983.

———. "Science Grapples with the Creative Puzzle." *New York Times*. May 13, 1984.

van Gogh, V. *The Letters of Vincent van Gogh*, edited and introduced by Mark Roskill. New York: Atheneum, 1963.

Goldsmith, O. *Comparative Comedies, Present and Past*, edited by R. K. Keyes and H. M. Roth. New York: Noble and Noble, 1957.

Hugo, V. M. *Les Misérables*. Paris: Garnier-Flammarion, 1967.

Huxley, T. H. *T. H. Huxley on Education*. Introductory Essay and Notes by C. Bibby. Cambridge, England: Cambridge University Press, 1971.

*The Kasidah of Haji Abdu El-Yezdi*. Translated and annotated by Sir Richard F. Burton. New York: Citadel Press, 1965.

Keats, J. *The Poetical Works of John Keats*, edited by H. Buxton Forman. London: Oxford University Press, 1937.

Kindler, H. S. "The Influence of a Meditation-Relaxation Technique on Group Problem-Solving Effectiveness." *Dissertation Abstracts International* 39 (7-A) (1979): 4370–4371.

Machiavelli, N. *The Prince*. Translated by N. H. Thomson. New York: Grolier, 1971.

Melville, H. *Moby Dick; or, The Whale*. Chicago: Encyclopaedia Britannica, 1952.

Milton, J. *Areopagitica*. New York: Collier, 1961.

Moore, G. A. *Confessions of a Young Man*. New York: Modern Library, 1925.

Morley, J. M. *The Life of William Ewart Gladstone*. New York: Macmillan, 1903.

Murphy, T. P. "Eureka." *Forbes Magazine*, May 7, 1984, 218.

"Neurologist Insists That Music, As Well As Life, Can Begin When One Is Forty." *New York Times*. July 13, 1986.

Pelletier, K. R. *Healthy People in Unhealthy Places*. New York: Delta/Seymour Lawrence, 1985.

Poe, E. A. *Essays and Reviews*. New York: Viking, 1984.

Pope, A. *The Complete Poetical Works of Alexander Pope*. Boston: Houghton Mifflin, 1902.

Sabel, B. A. "Transcendental Meditation and Concentration Ability." *Perceptual and Motor Skills* 50 (1980): 799–802.

Shakespeare, W. *The Complete Works of William Shakespeare*. New York: W. J. Black, 1937.

Spinoza, B. B. *Ethics*. Chicago: Encyclopaedia Britannica, 1952.

Spragins, E. E. "For Foote Cone, The Answer Is Still 'Whole-Brain' Thinking." *Business Week*, March 3, 1986, 120–121.

"Stress on the Job Cited." *New York Times*. October 23, 1986.

Tennyson, A. *The Poetical Works of Tennyson*, edited by G. R. Strange. Boston: Houghton Mifflin, 1974.

da Vinci, L. Selections from the *Note-books of Leonardo da Vinci*, edited by I. A. Richter. London: Oxford University Press, 1952.

Whitehead, A. N. *Dialogues of Alfred North Whitehead*. Boston: Little, Brown, 1954.

Yerkes, R. M., and Dodson, J. D. "The Relaxation of Strength of Stimulus to Rapidity of Habit Formation." *Journal of Comparative Neurology and Psychology* 18 (1908): 459–482.

Wilson, F. R. *Tone Deaf and All Thumbs? An Invitation to Music Making for Late Bloomers and Non-Prodigies*. New York: Viking, 1986.

*Chapter* **8.**

Ashbrook, J. B. "Brain, Mind and God." *The Christian Century*, March 19–26, 1986, 295–298.

Becker, E. *The Denial of Death*. New York: Free Press, 1973.

Benson, H. *Beyond the Relaxation Response*. New York: Times Books, 1984.

———. *The Relaxation Response*. New York: William Morrow, 1975.

Clifford, T. "Shirley MacLaine's Spiritual Dance." *American Health*, January–February, 1987, 52–53.

Dean, S. R. "Metapsychiatry: The Confluence of Psychiatry and Mysticism." In *Psychiatry and Mysticism*, edited by S. R. Dean. Chicago: Nelson-Hall, 1975.

*Gilgamesh*. Translated by J. Gardner and J. Maier. New York: Vintage Books, 1985.

Homer. *The Iliad*. Translated by R. Fitzgerald. Garden City, New York: Anchor Press, Doubleday, 1974.

James, W., in *In Search of White Crows*, by R. Laurence Moore. New York: Oxford University Press, 1977.

Jaynes, J. *The Origin of Consciousness and the Breakdown of the Bicameral Mind.* Boston: Houghton Mifflin, 1977.

Lindsey, R. "Gurus Hired to Motivate Workers Are Raising Fear of 'Mind Control.' " *New York Times,* April 17, 1987.

"The Lost Voices of the Gods." *Time Magazine,* March 14, 1977, 51–53.

Mandell, A. J. "Toward Psychobiology of Transcendence: God in the Brain." In *The Psychogiology of Consciousness,* edited by R. J. Davidson and J. M. Davidson. New York: Plenum, 1980.

## *Chapter* 9.

Benson, H. *Beyond the Relaxation Response.* New York: Times Books, 1984.

———. *The Mind/Body Effect.* New York: Simon and Schuster, 1979.

———. *The Relaxation Response.* New York: William Morrow, 1975.

Benson, H., and McCallie, D. P., Jr. "Angina Pectoris and the Placebo Effect." *New England Journal of Medicine* 300 (1979): 1424–1429.

Dean, S. R. "Metapsychiatry: The Confluence of Psychiatry and Mysticism." In *Psychiatry and Mysticism,* edited by S. R. Dean. Chicago: Nelson-Hall, 1975.

Goddard, G., and Douglas, R. "Does the Engram of Kindling Model the Engram of Long-Term Memory?" In *Kindling,* edited by J. A. Wada and R. T. Ross. New York: Raven Press, 1976.

Goodwin, D. W. *Anxiety*. New York: Oxford University Press, 1986.

Pert, C. B., et al. "Neuropeptides and Their Receptors: A Psychosomatic Network." *Journal of Immunology* 135 (1985): 820S–826S.

Post, R. "Stress Sensitization, Kindling and Conditioning." *Behavioral and Brain Sciences* 8 (1985): 372–373.

Racine, R.; Tuff, L.; and Zaide, J. "Kindling, Unit Discharge Patterns and Neural Plasticity." In *Kindling*, edited by J. A. Wada and R. T. Ross. New York: Raven Press, 1976.

Skolnick, P., and Paul, S. M. "New Concepts in the Neurobiology of Anxiety." *The Journal of Clinical Psychiatry* 44 (1983): 12–20.

Snyder, S. H. "Drug and Neurotransmitter Receptors in the Brain." *Science* 224 (1984): 22–31.

Squire, L. R. "Mechanisms of Memory." *Science* 232 (1986): 1612–1619.

# Index

ABOUT THE AUTHORS

**Herbert Benson**, M.D., a graduate of Wesleyan University and Harvard Medical School, is associate professor of medicine at the Harvard Medical School and chief of the Section on Behavioral Medicine at the New England Deaconess Hospital. He is the author of more than a hundred original scientific articles and the books: *The Relaxation Response*, *The Mind/Body Effect*, and *Beyond the Relaxation Response*.

**William Proctor**, a graduate of Harvard College and Harvard Law School, has written more than forty books, many of them on medical, scientific or religious subjects. Currently based in New York City, he and his author wife, Pam, are working on a number of projects, including the parenting of their son, Michael.